Seeing Beyond the Wrinkles

Seeing Beyond the Wrinkles

Stories of Ageless Courage, Humor, and Faith

Charles Tindell

Second Edition

Studio 4 Productions
Northridge, California

SEEING BEYOND THE WRINKLES
Stories of Ageless Courage, Humor, and Faith

© 1998, 1999 by Studio 4 Productions
All rights reserved
First Printing 1998
Second Printing 1999 (second edition, revised and expanded)

Studio 4 Productions
P.O. Box 280400
Northridge, CA 91328-0400
U.S.A.

ISBN: 1-882349-04-0

Library of Congress Catalog Card Number: 98-61477

Editor: Bob Rowland
Book Design: Carey Christensen
Cover Design: Robert Aulicino

Dedicated to the elderly whose wit and wisdom so often go untapped and whose daily acts of courage and faith go unnoticed. Only when we are able to see beyond their wrinkles will our own lives be enriched. For then, we will see them for who they really are and the gifts they have to offer.

Youth has a beautiful face and old age, a beautiful soul.

Swedish Proverb

Contents
(stories are grouped thematically)

Preface x

Stereotypes
Marjory 1
Seeing Beyond the Wrinkles 5
Violet 8
Mabel 11
Uniqueness
Lillian 13
Minnie 17
Opal 20
Lewis 23
Role Models
Hattie 27
Maybelle 29
Selma 32
Joyfulness
Clara 35
Anabel 37
Pearl 39
Sherman 42
Wisdom
Bill 45
Amen Corner 47
Vivienne 52
Ben 55
Love
Walter 58
Huddling 61
George 64
Isabelle 67
Fortitude
Ruby 70

Fortitude (cont.)

Ivah 73

Soulmates 76

Being a Parent 79

Friendship

Jewell 81

Ellen 85

August 87

Roscoe and Wallace 91

Caring

Two Nurses 94

Hector 97

Anna 100

Estelle and Leo 103

Storytellers

Wilbur 108

Gladys 111

Merle 115

Listening

Theodore 119

Rose 123

Esther 125

Frank 128

Memories

Carl 131

Orville 135

Reminiscing 137

The Snowman 140

Gifts

Almeda 143

Agnes 145

Lydia 148

Alma 151

Looking Back

I Wonder if I Know 154

Arthur 157

Looking Back (cont.)

    Edgar 161

The Journey

    Joseph 163

    Ruth 166

    Wilma 169

    Gilbert 172

Saying Good-bye

    Bess 175

    John 178

    Walfred 183

    Betty 186

Going Home

    Emma 189

    Marilla, Eben, and Otto 192

    Clifford 195

    Ebert 197

    Harry 201

Angels

    Cecil 204

    Jacob 207

    Beatrice 211

    Six Words 215

A Final Thought from the Author 217

Preface

You may be surprised to learn that the setting for these stories is a nursing home. While names and other particulars have been changed to safeguard the privacy of the individuals profiled here, the stories are based on true-life experiences.

These stories serve a threefold purpose. First, they capture the triumph of the ageless human spirit as defined in such attributes as love, caring, faith, and courage. In that sense, they are inspirational. Second, they are insightful. They not only provide insights into the elderly but also help us reflect upon our own aging process. Third, the stories are challenging. They challenge us to take a second look at ingrained stereotypes of nursing home residents in particular and the elderly in general, or, as one resident told me, "to see beyond the wrinkles."

This book can be appreciated by those who have an older person in their lives, be they young people with grandparents or caregivers whose relatives and friends are in their retirement years. It can also be enjoyed by the elderly themselves. As Joe, who lives in a nursing home and who claims to be "94 years young," said after reading the stories, "I have learned to know my neighbors here at the nursing home in a way I previously did not know them. Some of the stories made me cry and some made me laugh."

One question that often comes up when I am asked about working in a nursing home is, "Doesn't it get you down?" I believe that is the shorter version. The longer version of the question is, "Doesn't working with all those old people get you down?" This version is not usually asked because within it is the assumption that working at such a place would be depressing.

In order to examine this assumption more closely, I

ask that you consider the following exercise. Imagine two groups of people sitting and talking. The first is a group of young adults. Some are lounging about in comfortable chairs. Others are sitting on the floor, their backs supported by the wall. Now picture the second group of people. They are elderly residents in a nursing home. A few are in rockers but most are in wheelchairs. Would you expect both settings to be filled with laughter and wit? Or would you assume that only the young adults are capable of having a lively, happy, funny conversation? There seems to be a mindset that old people are lifeless and humorless. And why shouldn't they be, we ask? All they deal with is aging and the death process. Therefore, we conclude, they must lead a cheerless existence like once lively marionettes who now have nothing to do but sit around and complain that over the years their strings have become tangled and broken.

When asked how I like working in such a setting, my response is that I love it. I have observed two general characteristics of the people I have had the privilege to serve. The first is a positive attitude about life and the second, a sense of humor and wit. Such attributes, I suspect, are contributing factors to their longevity. The average age of the nursing home residents is eighty-five. In the years I have worked with them, I have enjoyed more laughter than I ever thought possible. Their wit and humor are, at times, incredible. So also are their strength, courage, and faith.

We should not forget that their stories will become our stories if we live long enough. If we can learn from them how they cope with the aging process, we will be better prepared to deal with our own aging. In many ways, in life and in death, they are our teachers. As you read on, judge for yourself.

Marjory

If ever there was an individual who fit the stereotypical image of a nursing home resident as a withered poor old soul whose last days are spent babbling away, Marjory certainly would have qualified. Outwardly, at least.

As she sat in the wheelchair, yelling and screaming, her demeanor was not all that inviting. My initial reaction was to avoid this person if I could. I knew, though, that because I was the chaplain, it was a visit that I would have to make. So I decided to go ahead and talk to her. Besides, I muttered to myself, I might as well get it over with and pray that the rest of the day would be more positive. Not exactly altruistic thoughts for a chaplain.

I slowly approached and hesitantly knelt down in front of Marjory so that we would be eye-to-eye, and said, "Hello, I am the Chaplain." I was prepared for just about anything, except her response. She stopped yelling, smiled, and replied in a pleasant-sounding voice, "Oh, it is so nice to meet you."

I think I recovered quickly enough from my surprise that Marjory was not aware of how dumbfounded I was. We proceeded to have a rational conversation, with her telling me about her religious experiences as a young woman. She asked me questions about myself and my work. She talked about aging and explained some of the physical problems she had had in recent years. She also shared her love of music and how she had played the piano. All in all, it was a most pleasant conversation. I thanked her for the visit and left. I had walked no more than twenty feet away when Marjory started yelling and screaming again.

The experience of walking into a nursing home and hearing people yelling, while also seeing shriveled bodies listing to one side in wheelchairs, is enough for some people to want to turn around and go right back out the door. This can be especially true when it is an initial visit. I know of people who simply cannot bring themselves to visit a nursing home because they get so depressed. One individual told me that she stopped coming because all she did was cry when she left.

I am sure there are many reasons why people do not like to visit nursing homes, but I suspect one of the main reasons is that it can be a vivid reminder of one's own aging process. It forces us to come face-to-face with the possibility that we may end up in similar circumstances. And, of course, we have all kinds of images we have carried around over the years. We all have heard "those stories" about those poor old people. We tend to carry these unpleasant stereotypes with us when we visit. Unfortunately, they oftentimes keep us from getting close to residents like Marjory.

One of the worst ways, in my opinion, to experience a nursing home is to simply walk down the hallway. That can feel as if you are walking an emotional gauntlet, beset on both sides by unpleasant sights and pitiful sounds. The drawback is that we make the setting more impersonal than it actually is while reinforcing our own negative, and often fearful, stereotypes of the elderly nursing home resident.

It is only when we see a resident as a person that we take the risk of engaging them. More often than not, when we do, we are surprised and will certainly be pleased by their ability to engage us. We need to be sensitive to the level on which engagement takes place. We may, for example, converse with one resident as we would with anyone else. With another, it may be simply allowing them to reach out and touch our arm or hold our hand. I have been with residents who were unable to communicate verbally but they let their feelings known with facial expressions or eye movements. Being in a wheelchair does not mean one no longer uses body language. Each resident, regardless of physical or mental condition, has a distinctive personality and an individuality. Such individuals should not be seen as "the guy who was drooling" or the "old thing that looked like a bag of bones" or "the one who did all the yelling."

The next time you visit a nursing home, I encourage you to leave any stereotypes you may have at the door. You can always pick them up as you leave.

You may be wondering: Why did Marjory yell and scream? I am not entirely sure, but I remember she once said she was a person who was impatient and really did not like to wait. If I spent my time in a wheelchair, waiting to converse with people who picked up their pace as they walked past me, I might feel like yelling and screaming also.

Seeing Beyond the Wrinkles

Shopping at a mall the other day, I stopped to look at some hand puppets. A salesman, who must have been in his late twenties, was demonstrating them. He had the puppet say, "Hi, Pops. How are you doing?" At first I wasn't sure who was being addressed. I looked behind me to see if anyone was there. Then it dawned on me that he was talking to me. My first thought was, Who was he to call me "Pops"? Then I realized that he was relating to me only on the basis of my age. I could tell, unfortunately for us both, that he never got that stereotype out of his mind as he talked to me.

That evening, as I thought further about my encounter, I wondered if many people relate to others simply on the basis of their age and physical appearance. If that is true, then I believe those who do are really missing out on something, especially as they deal with older persons. If they look at the elderly and see only gray hair or wrinkly skin—if they notice nothing other than their use of walkers or canes or that they are in wheelchairs or that they can't see or hear very well—if that is the only way they see and relate to them, then, unfortunately, everyone misses an enriching human encounter.

I recall visiting a resident who was very upset. She was crying and said that she had had some visitors who treated her in a patronizing way. With tears running down her face and anger in her voice, she cried out, "Why can't they see past the wrinkles?" She, like so many her age, is fighting stereotypes. The experience inspired this poem:

Worn and faded by the years, she sat on the bed
    And asked

"Why do they see just the wrinkles?
    Why?"
Startled, I looked beyond the flesh
    And when I did, I saw in her eyes
The playfulness of a girl,
    The inquisitiveness of a young lady,
The wisdom of a woman,
    A daughter of God.
I listened to her words and as I left,
    I looked once more
And this time, I saw God's child.

Violet

Have you ever lain on your back on a summer day and looked up at the cloud shapes, trying to imagine faces or animals in them? If you have, read on; I want to tell you about Violet.

Violet is confined to a wheelchair and is in almost constant pain. One day I noticed she was looking at what appeared to be bruises on her arms. Both arms and the backs of her hands were covered with black-and-blue marks. In the elderly, the slightest bump will cause weakening blood vessels to rupture.

As we talked, Violet looked over the bruises and just shook her head, saying, "It is hard to believe these arms and hands are part of me. It is like standing outside of myself and looking at this person sitting in the wheelchair."

It was not self-pity or sadness she was expressing, but more of an incredulous curiosity. All of us, I think, can identify with what she was experiencing. We all have had the same feeling when we have gotten up in the morning, looked in the mirror and wondered who that person was staring back at us.

There are many nursing home residents whose minds and attitudes are as energetic as those who are chronologically younger but whose physical bodies, unfortunately, are not. I believe the negative stereotype depicting the elderly as unable to grasp new concepts and changes in the world has been reinforced by sayings like, "You can't teach an old dog new tricks." It has been my experience that there are many oldsters who are just as capable of understanding new ideas and expressing creativity and imagination as anyone else. While it may be true that there are those who cannot name the current president of the United States, it is equally true that there are those who are as up-to-date with current critical issues as anyone half their age.

One of the more lively conversations I have had was with a 102-year-old woman who felt strongly that the current political climate was far too conservative in terms of women's rights. On another occasion, a resident described how we have passed from the Industrial Age to the Digital Age and how it will be a period in which young people will need to be open to constant change. She was addressing her remarks to the members of the younger generation who had come to celebrate her 100th birthday.

Recently, several computers were purchased for the residents' library. A sign-up sheet for computer lessons was quickly filled with the names of eager residents. Whenever I walk past and see them sitting at the computers, I can't help but laugh at the assertion, "You can't teach an old dog new tricks."

When I came upon Violet that day, looking so intently at those bruises on her arms and hands, I asked her what she was thinking. She looked up at me with an impish smile and said, "I was trying to identify animals and faces. You know, like you do with clouds in the sky."

Mabel

Mabel spoke three languages and, in younger days, had been a worldwide traveler. On one visit, she expressed her views on religions of the world while asking me to explain the difference between the Koran and the Christian Bible. During another visit, with a note of disgust, she commented on the sad state of politics and how she felt politicians should read the Constitution before trying to pass laws that undermine an individual's basic rights. She was talking about some piece of legislation of which I had no knowledge. On one of our last visits before she died, she wanted to talk about the theology of the Eucharist; specifically, the Roman Catholic doctrine of transubstantiation as opposed to the Protestant doctrine of consubstantiation. The last time I heard anyone use that terminology was in seminary.

I always think of Mabel when people assume that talking with "the old people" must get a little boring. Nursing home residents are all too aware of the image people have of them. As one woman in her eighties said, "People think that all us old people ever do at the home is rock in our rocking chairs and talk about our aches and pains."

It may surprise some to know that many of the residents, though their bodies are declining physically, have minds that are still active and alert. Not only can they talk about the current world situation, they can do most of us one better. They can also compare it to life as it was years ago, not from books they have read but from having lived through that period of history.

All my conversations with Mabel took place in her room as she lay resting in her bed; she was often so weak, she could not sit very long in her wheelchair. But then again, what would you expect from someone who was nearly 102 years old?

Lillian

"Why do you waste your time with us?" I have been asked many questions over the years, but this was a first. It was asked by a ninety-six-year-old woman named Lillian. Her hands are crippled by arthritis, and her life consists of being confined to either a bed or a wheelchair, except at those times when she is able to sit in a recliner rocker by the window in her room. She is a woman of strong faith, but I think her question may reflect an all too common attitude within our society about putting degrees of value on human beings, depending upon who they are and how significant the world determines them to be. Among far too many, the prevailing attitude about elderly people in nursing homes seems to be that they are just marking time to die. Since they are no longer considered productive and are "on their way out," their value index is not very high. To those who argue that many of the elderly themselves believe this, one could counter that perhaps they are just living up to the expectations placed upon them. If a group of people is continually being given the message that they are "valueless," they will begin to believe and act as if it is so.

It seems ironic that one is able to find more theological questioning and wrestling with the profound spiritual questions of life on the comic pages than in any other section of the newspaper. I frequently look at a Calvin and Hobbes cartoon strip on my bulletin board, particularly when I come up against a question such as the one Lillian asked. For those who may not be familiar with the classic cartoon strip, it portrayed the antics of a little boy named Calvin and his stuffed toy tiger, Hobbes. In the first frame of the comic strip on my bulletin board, Calvin is outside. It is evening, and he is looking up into the night sky at all the stars.

In the second frame, as he continues to look up at the endless dark void, he yells, "I'm Significant!" The third frame shows him silently staring up into the darkness. The final frame has Calvin saying in a meek voice, "screamed the dust speck."

I wonder how many of us feel like a "dust speck" at times. It is so easy to get into the rut of feeling that our lives do not mean much in the scheme of creation. This feeling of insignificance is thrust upon groups of people: women are not seen as "significant" when compared to men; people of color are not seen as "significant" when compared to "white" people; homeless people are not seen as "significant enough" to really do something about, and so on. Unfortunately, this prejudice is also applied to people when they get older, as if to imply that only productive, younger people are significant. What does this say, then, to those who live into their eighties and nineties and whose days are spent in wheelchairs, needing assistance for many of the simple daily tasks we do without thinking? Is it any wonder Lillian asks her question?

Instead of listening to the world as to who is and who is not significant, we might benefit by listening to some words written in the Bible. Let me paraphrase Psalm 8, verses 3-5:

When I look at the sky, which You have made, at the moon and the stars which You set in their places, Who are we, that You think of us, mere "dust specks," that You care for us? Yet You made us inferior only to Yourself, You crowned us with glory and honor.

Those words portray a spiritual truth that all people can affirm: every single one of us is significant because each of us is a unique creation. The statement, "They broke the mold when they made so and so," may be a cliché, but it is one that is true for all of us. We are to celebrate individuals for who they are and not simply for their productivity or their pragmatic value in meeting the needs of society. It may be true that all of us, like Lillian, will collect the "dust of the ages" over the years, but none of us is a "dust speck."

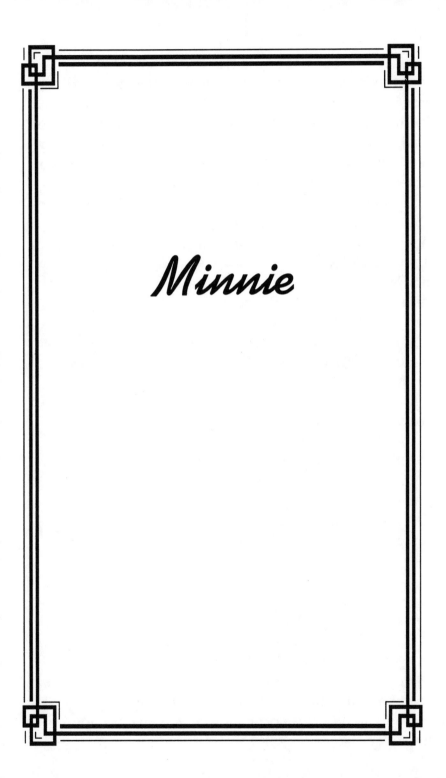

Minnie

Minnie was cussing up a storm. "I'm going to get my lawyer.... This place is a jail... not fit for human habitation.... Where am I, anyway?.... A dog shouldn't have to live here.... My family just dropped me off and left me.... Wait until I tell them how they treat me here.... Get me out of here...."

It was Minnie's first day at the nursing home, and she was angry. Her family had left an hour before, having been unsuccessful in their attempt to calm her. They had stayed and talked with her for nearly four hours. Throughout the whole time they sat with her during the noon meal, they were encouraging her to eat and attempting to convince her that the staff was not trying to poison her. Minnie would not eat nor would she lie down in a bed. She was sure she would be strapped down in it until she died. The family's final comment to the staff as they left was, "We're sorry."

Staff members had tried to calm Minnie as well, but to no avail. When I came upon the scene, the staff were respectfully keeping their distance from this "ninety-one-year-old fireball in a wheelchair." They decided it would be best to let her have her own space for awhile. They would offer her something to eat later.

"Chaplain, why don't you see what you can do," an aide asked, as she glanced over my shoulder at Minnie coming down the hall in our direction.

"Sure," I answered, somewhat confidently.

With several of the staff watching, I went up to Minnie, knelt down in front of her and said, with a friendly smile and the most pleasant sounding tone of voice I had, "Good morning, Minnie. How are you doing today?"

Wheeling up to within inches of me and then looking me straight in the eye, Minnie yelled,

"And who the hell are you?"

Somewhat daunted, but also being aware of the giggling of some of the housekeepers who had looked up from their work to observe the scene unfolding, I decided to pull out "my ace in the hole" and said, "I am the Chaplain."

Minnie, unimpressed, replied, "So what?" and wheeled past, leaving me sitting on my haunches in the middle of the corridor. She continued her litany: "I'm getting my lawyer.... This place is no good.... Just wait until my family finds out how they are treating me...."

Extricating myself as painlessly as I could after being consoled by the staff, I walked back to my office. On my way I happened to pass the employee time clock and saw that it had a handwritten sign taped to it. I stopped to read it. It said "Out of Order." With real clarity, it told me what I was feeling and inspired these thoughts:

Passing by one day
A sign caught my eye.
"Out of Order," it simply said.
I stopped and pondered.
"Out of Order," it said.
Removing it, I put it upon myself
And walked away.

If you are ever having a day when you feel things are just not working as they should, I have a well-worn sign you could borrow.

Opal

Opal showed me a picture of herself in a one-piece bathing suit taken on a beach, the name of which she has long since forgotten. At the time, she was a young woman of eighteen. Though that was over seventy years ago, she has kept the photograph.

Handing it back to her, I told her, "Opal, you know, today you would be called a 'cute chick.'" Her initial reaction was one of laughter. However, she looked at the picture again and said, "Really. Do you think so?"

"Yes, I do."

Opal closed her eyes for a moment, and then looked at me and smiled somewhat wistfully. For the next twenty minutes or so, she shared memories of those years. Of the "suitors" who came calling and the wonderful times she had. Of picnics and new dances to learn.

Memories let others know who we have been and what we have done, lest they think what they presently see is the full picture. That is why we hold a short, informal observance called a Service of Remembrance whenever a resident dies. Since it is not meant to take the place of a formal memorial or funeral service, it is not held in the chapel but rather in a location on the particular floor where the resident lived. The service lasts no longer than one-half hour, and families are told that staff may come and go as they need to because of their duties. The primary purpose is to provide closure for other residents, staff, and family. The observance also serves an important secondary purpose.

Family members are encouraged to bring youthful pictures of the person who has died. They may also bring other items that tell us about the person. One family brought a beautiful afghan, which their mother had made when she was in her twenties. Another family brought three oil paintings by their father. Another, some of their father's writings. The photographs, along with other items, are important because they serve to provide staff and other residents a broader picture of who this person was whom we got to know only in later years.

At the service, after a brief reading centered on the theme that each of us is uniquely created by God, those present are asked to share stories and memories. Family members are asked to share stories of the person, especially when he or she was younger. It is eye-opening for staff to hear that the person who had been confined to a wheelchair for the past several years once played basketball for a girls' high school team. Or that someone who had to be fed because her hands were too crippled by arthritis once produced beautiful, detailed needlework.

These services let the residents know that they will be remembered, not only as individuals who lived in a nursing home but for their full lives. There have been residents who have been personally influenced by attending. They had thought they would have no services of any kind because they really did not want a formal funeral. Since participating in Services of Remembrance, and liking the informal gathering and sharing of stories, they have chosen that option. More than that, however, they have sensed the importance of remembering and of being remembered as having lived a life before coming to the home.

When that time comes for Opal, I plan to encourage her family to show pictures of her as a young woman especially the picture of her on that beach.

Lewis

Lewis is a very interesting and delightful individual. He can be charming and witty and has proven to be quite the catalyst for initiating a conversation on just about any subject you care to mention. One needs to be prepared, however, for you never know what subject he is going to talk about and especially, how he will introduce it.

One afternoon, for example, I happened to be walking through the unit in which he is a resident. Lewis, who cannot sit still very long, was up pacing. He was about ten or fifteen feet ahead of me. Before I could catch up to him, he stopped in front of a couple of women who were sitting and talking. I thought to myself, "Hmmmmm. I wonder what old Lewis is up to now."

"Malarkey!" Lewis blurted out, somewhat startling the two ladies.

At first I thought perhaps he was giving a commentary on whatever they were talking about and, if so, I hoped this was not going to evolve into some kind of scene. Although Lewis can be witty, there is sometimes a fine line between what he considers to be witty and what others might perceive as sarcasm. Before either of the women could reply, Lewis smiled and added, "Bet you haven't heard that word for awhile!"

The two women looked at one another and then back at Lewis as they nodded their heads approvingly, with one speaking for both. "You're right on that. And you know, it is such a good word."

Using the word malarkey as a beginning point, the three of them went on to discuss a number of other words and expressions that are rarely heard in everyday conversation. As I went on my way, they were talking about the expression, "Greetings and salutations," and how much more elegant it is than the current, "Hi, how are you?" The two ladies seemed to be thoroughly enjoying themselves. As I mentioned, Lewis can be quite a charming conversationalist.

Lewis, within his circumstances, tries to lead as full a life as he is able. He sings in the resident choir, goes to most of the scheduled activities (his favorite is word games), listens to classical music and, most importantly, tries to keep his mind as alert and active as possible. The latter is very important to him because he knows he is, as he says, "losing it." This is not just a case of the occasional memory loss that all of us experience and joke about as we get older; it is exactly what Lewis is saying. He is "losing it," and he knows it.

The diagnosis written on Lewis' chart is "Dementia/Alzheimer's." Although he has never used the "A" word in conversations with me, he realizes that he is not the man he used to be. When he was in the work force, Lewis was a highly respected educator. His insights on complex issues were widely sought by his peers. Though he is battling the effects of Alzheimer's, Lewis continues to make insightful comments. During one worship service, for example, I made the statement, "Each of us matters to God." Lewis came up to me afterwards and said, "Wouldn't it be nice if God mattered to each of us. It would be a much better world."

One might wonder if Lewis is a typical Alzheimer's resident. There is an old saying among staff who work with such individuals: When you have seen one person with Alzheimer's, you have seen one person with Alzheimer's. Though Lewis may indeed be "losing it," he is not giving in without a fight. He is an example of the courage of the human spirit struggling against impossible odds. Lewis is simply one example of someone who has Alzheimer's.

Certainly those with Alzheimer's need our care, compassion, understanding, and love. But also, they need our respect for them as individuals at whatever their stage of the disease. All Alzheimer's residents are not alike. In fact, no two are alike. If anyone assumes they are, there is a certain word Lewis would like to tell you about.

Hattie

I was called to the third floor of the Chronic Care building to see Hazel, who had had a stroke that morning. She was in a double room. The curtain divider was drawn for her privacy. Other than her roommate, Hattie, who was on the other side of the curtain, there was no one else in the room. Although Hazel seemed to be resting comfortably, the prognosis, I had been told, was not very good. As it turned out, she died three days later.

I spoke her name, but there was no response. After a short prayer, I decided to stay for awhile and figure out what else I could do. As I sat down, I saw there was a card on her dresser that told me that this day was her birthday. I thought to myself, "What a lousy way to spend a birthday."

I spoke up and said, "Hazel, it is your birthday today."

No sooner had I spoken than a voice from the other side of the curtain started singing, "Happy birthday to you, happy birthday to you...."

I peeked around the curtain and there was ninety-nine-year-old Hattie, lying in bed, a smile on her face, and singing for all she was worth.

No one had to tell Hattie what else could be done.

Maybelle

Her favorite comment to me was, "Grandpa always said that it's heck to get old." Sitting by the elevator, Maybelle watched people walk by day after day. Was she lonely? Maybe. But I have a hunch that Maybelle had another objective.

Maybelle worked at a Veteran's Hospital after World War Two and in describing her work, she always talked about her "boys." She said that some of the staff would chide her about spending so much time with the patients. Her reply was that the boys needed a friend, and she always took the time to talk and visit with them because it was important. As she told me this, her eyes were looking directly into mine and were amazingly steady considering they had been in use for over ninety-seven years. My impression is that Maybelle was not so much looking for a response as she was making sure I was hearing the message that caring for others is what life is all about. No doubt, each time she had this encounter with someone, she was in her own way teaching the finer points of caring for others.

If one were to come upon Maybelle sitting in her favorite spot, the initial impression might be that she was asleep or lost in her own thoughts. But upon further observation, you would see her suddenly perk up whenever someone walked by. Her eyes would alertly follow until after the person was out of sight. Then she would once again resume the appearance of sleeping or dozing. When that observation is linked with the story she always told of her "boys," one understands that she was indeed sizing people up, checking to see if they would stop to say hello. In her working days, she always stopped to say hello to her "boys," even though it was not her job. Maybelle was not a professional caregiver as some might think but rather a housekeeping aide. Yet she probably did as much caregiving as those whose jobs were to be caregivers. Knowing her, I suspect she did so because she believed that to live life means to care for and love others.

You might be interested in knowing that two days after she died, another staff member related to me that, for the chaplain, Maybelle had always softened Grandpa's comment. To others, she quoted what he really said. I figure this was just another example of her caregiving. In this case, she was taking care of the chaplain.

Selma

She was not doing so badly for, as she described herself, "an old lady." When asked how old she was, she would laugh and say, "I'm old enough to know everything!"

Selma depended on a walker to get around because of a chronic back condition, and she had a hearing problem; still, she felt she was in fairly good condition. Getting involved in as many different activities as she could, from popcorn ball making to ceramics, and volunteering for one project or another, she managed to keep quite busy. "Who says you have to spend your life rocking in a rocking chair?" she would say. One of her favorite pastimes was socializing with her many friends. She loved to play cards and could play cribbage with the best of them. "Life is to be lived!" she would say, and her plan was to keep going as long as she could. Then she had her stroke.

Selma has had extensive physical and speech therapy since the stroke and has made some progress, but the future does not look promising. The effects of the stroke on her social life have been the most difficult. One can see the frustration in her eyes when she tries to express complete thoughts but is not able. Her days are now spent in a wheelchair, watching television by herself. If asked the reason why her friends don't come around very much anymore, Selma will explain, "People... ah... impatient... er... er... me."

It is true that Selma's friends seldom come to visit with her, but we must be careful not to judge them too harshly. If staff people have a hard time communicating with her, just imagine how difficult it is for those who are not trained to deal with stroke patients. Besides that, their own hearing and vision impairments would only add to the anxiety and frustration involved in any attempts at communication. As one friend commented, "I get so nervous because of my hearing, and I am afraid I wouldn't hear the words she was saying. I think it would only make her more frustrated."

Having had such a full, active life, Selma might be expected to feel anger and bitterness because of what has happened to her. No one would blame her for having such feelings. Though she does admit to having them, there is another feeling that comes across in a powerful way. One that reflects who she is.

Some of the first words she expressed after weeks of therapy were, "Er... I... er... ah... sympathy... er... more... for... ah... those... er... er... who... er... ah... ah... strokes."

Clara

Clara hangs on to the book as though her life depends upon it. It is always on the tray attached to her wheelchair. Having very poor eyesight, she bends over to read it until it seems as though she will touch it with her nose. In order to talk to her, one has to literally shout because of her hearing loss. Consequently, Clara is left pretty much to herself, and it seems that as long as she has that book, she is content. Most of the time she is very quiet, as if she is in her own little world. Most of the time.

It is not uncommon for Clara to break into a song at what some might consider inappropriate times. She can start singing, for example, when someone is in the middle of giving a talk to the group of residents of which she is a part or at the noon meal. Her musical outbursts can interrupt her tablemates in midsentence. More than once I have had to compete with her as I gave the blessing for a meal.

Clara is simply not aware of interrupting others because of her hearing problem. The other residents have come to accept that she may start singing at any time. They understand, and though she can be a little disruptive, they still want her to be included in the group. When she does start singing in her off-key, gravelly voice, repeating but one line over and over again, they smile.

"Jesus loves me, this I know, for the Bible tells me so... Jesus loves me, this I know, for the Bible tells me so... Jesus loves me, this I know...."

Anabel

Anabel motioned for me to come over. "I have a joke to tell you," she said. "A friend called this morning to tell it to me. I think you'll enjoy it."

I did. It was a funny story, and I laughed so hard that some of the other residents, as well as the staff, took notice. I remember thinking, I hope they do not misunderstand what is going on. In order to explain what I mean, as well as to try to capture the mood of the moment, I'll tell the story Anabel shared with me.

An eighty-year-old woman arrived home from the hospital with the new baby she had given birth to several days earlier. She wasn't in her house more than an hour when the front doorbell rang. It was her next door neighbor who had come over to see the baby. She invited the neighbor in, and they chatted over a cup of tea. After awhile, the neighbor said, "I really have to get back. May I see your baby?" The new mother replied, "Yes, of course, but you will have to wait until he cries. I can't remember where I put him down!"

Anabel is ninety-four years old. Her friend who called that morning is ninety years old. Both could identify with the woman in the story and her short-term memory loss. Many who are experiencing the decline of their physical and mental capacities do find the humor in that which comes with growing older. In my opinion, they have earned the right to laugh together over such things. In sharing the joke together, they are sharing the humor that they see within their world. By sharing it with me, Anabel was inviting me to enter that world and laugh, not at them, but with them.

Pearl

You would have liked Pearl. For being 102 years old, she had a great sense of humor. At her 100th birthday party, she made it a point to take me to meet her "baby" sister. Her sister was ninety-seven years old and just as lively as Pearl. On another occasion, I was walking by a sitting area that happened to have a couch, and there was Pearl stretched out with her eyes closed, a book resting on her chest. I stopped for a moment and just as I did, she opened her eyes and said, with a lilt in her voice, "Bet you thought I was dead!"

Pearl had a zest for living and a strong, lively faith. She was convinced that one of the attributes of God had to be laughter. "After all," she would say, "doesn't the Bible talk about rejoicing?" She frequently would clip out jokes and send them to me, no doubt making sure that the chaplain did some rejoicing in his life. I would like to share a story she told me. It was, as she said, "my all-time favorite story."

Granny was eighty-nine years old. She had only three teeth left and they were getting bad, so her doctor put her in the hospital to have them removed. Next day the preacher came to visit Granny. Sitting by her hospital bed was a large bowl of peanuts, and the minister started chowing down on the nuts while he was visiting with his elderly parishioner. When he had consumed the entire bowl of nuts, he became quite embarrassed and told Granny, "When I come back to see you, I'll bring you some more peanuts."

At that Granny flapped her gums and said, "Good, but be sure to get the kind with chocolate on them because all I can do is suck off the chocolate and spit the nuts into that bowl."

While the story is quite funny, especially if you can imagine it being told by a 102-year-old woman, it also makes an important statement. By telling it, Pearl wanted her listeners to know that the elderly can have and use humor as well as get the best of a younger person, even a minister. It is a story of triumph.

Pearl died two years ago and I miss her. She was living proof that the elderly can hold their own and do not have to take second place to anyone. She was also a living example of what the Bible means about rejoicing in our faith.

There are many things that I will remember about Pearl, but there is one thing I am really trying to recall: Was she the resident who once gave me some peanuts to eat?

Sherman

"We'll be glad when we all can boogie again."

Those words were uttered by Sherman, an 84-year-old resident who has had two hip replacements and can walk only with the aid of a walker. His mobility, though, is limited. He can walk about twenty feet before he needs to sit down. A month ago, he could do thirty to forty feet before sitting. "I get so tired now," he tells me, "and the pain is not good." His doctor has told him that within six months, he'll be in a wheelchair. Sherman merely shrugs his shoulders and motions with his hands as if to say "What can I do? There are some things you have no control over." Another hip replacement is out of the question because of Sherman's heart condition. As he sits resting in the chair, wondering if he can do another twenty feet, Sherman tells me that he has come to that point in his life where he'll have more bad days than good days. He says it matter-of-factly, without any sign that he is feeling sorry for himself. Sherman, like many of the other residents, has a realistic view of what's in store for him. He will tell you that he doesn't like the idea of getting old, but in the same breath he says, "You have to do what you have to do. If I have to be in a wheelchair, I'll be in a wheelchair then."

Sherman's remark about looking forward to boogying again had come after I had said a blessing for the noon meal and announced that today was the birthday of the composer who wrote the song, "Cow Cow Boogie." The mention of the song's name brought back memories for many residents, including Sherman, who said of days gone by that he could dance up a storm with the best of them. One of the women at his table spoke up and told us that when she was younger, she was the best jitterbug dancer around. Another woman at the next table began snapping her fingers as she swayed to musical memories. Sherman looked at the two women, and as he did, I had the feeling he was wondering what kind of dance partners they would have been.

Sherman's comment made about boogying was more than just about dancing. Knowing Sherman's deep spiritual beliefs, I believe his remark was a statement of his faith and the hope it gives him. There are many residents who, like Sherman, find a great deal of comfort and strength in their religious beliefs. "If it weren't for my trust in God, I don't know how I'd get through this," a resident told me when I visited her. This resident, a youthful-looking woman in her early 70s was injured in a car accident three years ago and is paralyzed from the waist down. Her faith keeps her going, even though she says, "Sometimes I can only deal with life five minutes at a time."

"Sherman, do you ever get discouraged?" I asked.

"Sure I do, Chaplain," he said. "Everybody does, don't they? I just tell myself that such is life, and I try to make the best of the situation. God will take care of me. After all, if you can't trust God, who can you trust?"

Residents like Sherman give verbal expression to their faith in many ways. One way, of course, is through the singing of hymns. They especially love to sing the old-time favorites such as "In the Garden" and "Amazing Grace." Another favorite is "When the Saints Go Marching In." And every time we sing it, I cannot help but think of Sherman because I suspect that when he sings it, he changes the word Marching to Boogying.

Bill

Failing eyesight, along with a recent hip replacement and a new hearing aid that does not seem to help, are just a few of the reasons Bill, twenty-three years beyond the age of retirement, says, "The Golden Years of retirement are a little tarnished."

There are few residents who would disagree with Bill's assessment of the retirement years. They are not so much bitter about it as they are simply expressing what they consider to be a realistic assessment of what the years do bring.

When we talk about "being real" in today's world, those in their eighties and nineties perhaps have more of a sense of reality about their stage of life than many of us who are younger and who are rushing toward "retirement."

As Bill says, "Don't rush getting old. Take life easy now." After overhearing staff members complain about some of their aches and pains, he smiled and said, "Old Age Benefits!"

Amen Corner

It's referred to as *"Amen Corner,"* and it's the spot where Sarah, Gaylord, and Bud can usually be found "hanging out " in their wheelchairs.

Amen Corner is an area on the second floor of the Chronic Care Center where two corridors come together to form a right angle. Residents like to gather there because they have a clear view in either direction and thus can (as they say), "Watch the world go by." Windows on the one outside wall allow the sun to shine in every afternoon. Sarah loves the spot because she can bask in the afternoon sun. "It warms my back," she once told me. "You know me and my poor circulation. I'm so cold all the time. I'd die without the sun."

As I stop to say hello to the three of them this afternoon I learn that Gaylord likes Amen Corner for another reason.

"It's a great place to watch people come and go," he says. "So many of them rush by. They don't seem to have much time for anything. Now, me," he chuckles, "I've got all the time in the world."

"Me too," Bud says. His wheelchair is adjacent to Gaylord's. "Ain't got much of anything but time, and I ain't got much of that left, either." He points to an armchair. "Chaplain, why don't you sit down for a while and watch the world go by with us."

"Thanks, I'll do that." I'm pleased that they have invited me to join their group. I decide not to mention, however, that I'm also one of those people who would have rushed by, since I was on my way to a meeting.

"Here she comes again," Gaylord announces as he motions toward a woman coming down the hallway in her wheelchair.

"Yep, and she's still singing," Bud adds.

The woman they are referring to seems dwarfed by her wheelchair; her feet barely touch the floor. As she wheels closer, we hear what's she singing. It's the same song she sang yesterday, and the day before that, and the day before that. "Bubbles, I'm forever blowing bubbles. Tiny bubbles. Tiny bubbles. Bubbles, I'm forever blowing bubbles, Tiny bubbles...." We smile and greet her. She pays no attention to us as she goes by. She is too engrossed in her singing. "Bubbles, I'm forever blowing bubbles...." The sound of her voice fades as she wheels farther away.

"I wonder why she sings that song all the time," Bud asks as he scratches the back of his head.

"Don't know," Gaylord replies. "Why don't you ask her the next time she comes around."

Bud grins, shakes his head, and whispers, "No."

Sarah opens her eyes, smiles, and then closes her eyes again. She doesn't seem to have a care in the world as she soaks in the warmth of the sun's rays. "I use to have a cat who would stretch out in the sun each afternoon," she says softly, her eyes still closed. "Now, I can appreciate what she was doing. In my next life, I think I'll be a cat."

Two staff persons hurry by, smile, and say hello. Before anyone in the group can reply, the two are halfway down the corridor.

"Pretty busy people," Bud says. "Too bad."

In the next few minutes we take in many sights and sounds. We watch an aide walking a resident who is groaning with each step he takes. Another aide is pushing a wheelchair right behind the groaning man in the event he suddenly decides to sit down. "I can't do it, I can't do it," the man says. "Yes, you can," the aide replies. "Just take a few more steps."

From the other direction, a man and a woman walk by. The woman is in tears. I overhear a portion of what she is saying, "Oh, she looks so fragile. What do you think we should do?" By the time the man answers, they are out of my hearing range.

The barking of a dog captures our attention. Even Sarah opens her eyes for a moment. A man with a golden retriever is coming in our direction. As they walk by, he stops to let Bud and Gaylord pet the dog which welcomes the attention. After the man and his dog move on, Bud says, "I used to have a dog like that. His name was Pete. He lived to be 15 years old. Then one day we found Pete out in the backyard. Old Pete just curled up and died."

"That's what I'm going to do one of these days," Gaylord says with a smile.

Bud looks at his friend and laughs.

I look at Sarah and wonder if she's sleeping. She looks so comfortable, I almost expect to hear sounds of purring. Just as I am about to get up from my chair to go to my meeting, LaVonne wheels up in her wheelchair. She's in her 90s. Six months ago, when she arrived at the nursing home, she was not expected to live more than a week.

"LaVonne, what are you up to today?" I ask.

"I'm taking my wheelchair around the world," she said. "Don't have time to sit and visit. See you later."

"I'm afraid I have to go also," I tell Bud and Gaylord. Sarah opens her eyes, nods, and then closes them again. As I walk away, I think to myself that, in a way, I *did* watch the world go by—the world of the residents. It's a most interesting and fascinating world, once you get to know it.

I suspect there's an Amen Corner in every nursing home or retirement center. If you are ever invited to sit awhile by those who are there, by all means, take the opportunity. You won't be sorry, for you have been invited into their world. And from that spot, you'll learn about life and death as you watch their world go by.

Vivienne

Vivienne will tell you she learned many lessons from her mother, who had to raise five children under the age of ten after her husband was killed in a car accident. Though during this time her mother had health problems, Vivienne says she was strong in other ways. "She taught me that we will have many aches and pains over the years but not to feel sorry for ourselves. Momma also would tell me, 'You got to be patient with life.'"

One would not have to be with Vivienne very long to understand that her mother's philosophy of "being patient with life" meant to face life with courage and not to give in to self-pity. Vivienne has had the opportunity to practice her mother's teachings over the past several years because of her own health problems. She was diagnosed with glaucoma and had to give up the reading she loved to do. Besides failing eyesight, Vivienne developed a chronic hip problem that permanently confined her to a wheelchair. In spite of these and other health concerns, she never complained but, instead, looked for new ways to live a fulfilling life. One way she accomplished that while embracing the sentiments of her mother was by listening to books recorded on tape. "I may not be able to read," she told me, "but I still can enjoy books."

Vivienne often speaks of other residents and is concerned about their problems. "Poor Laura," she says, "she cries all the time." or "Samuel came in last week and is so lonely." Vivienne does what she can to help. For Laura, she listens as they share a cup of tea. During their visits Laura's crying stops and one can even detect an occasional smile on her face. For Samuel, Vivienne has invited him to activities and other social gatherings, making sure he meets other residents. In both cases, Vivienne is, by example and words of encouragement, passing along her mother's philosophy about "being patient with life."

On a recent visit to Vivienne, she called my attention to a picture on the wall of her room showing a young man in an army uniform. The handsome soldier is smiling and looking directly into the camera. It is her son. She said he was killed during World War Two. "It was almost too much for me," she sighed, her eyes glistening, "but I remembered what Momma said." A long silence followed as Vivienne seemed to be revisiting the past. After a while she looked out her window at the construction going on. "I am going to miss those trees." She was referring to the trees marked for removal in order to make way for a building addition. I mistakenly assumed she was changing the subject until she added, "Momma always told me to be patient with life." She looked at her son's picture and then gazed again out the window. We both knew that the removal of trees would dramatically change her beautiful view and once again, life will call upon her to face the tomorrows with strength and courage. One may wonder if Vivienne, well into her eighties, can continue to deal with the many kinds of losses that one encounters in life.

We had visited for a while, and I was about to leave, when Vivienne said, "Well, I am going to go and visit now with Helen. She's my tablemate. Poor thing, she's had a slight stroke and seems to be down in the dumps."

As I watched Vivienne wheel down the hall, I could not help but think that her mother would be proud that her daughter is helping others learn what it means to be "patient with life."

Ben

Ben sought me out one afternoon and asked if I would stop by his room when I had some time. "Got something to show you," he said and then added, "God works in mysterious ways." My curiosity was sufficiently piqued, and so I went early the next morning after I knew he had finished breakfast.

The first thing he said to me was, "Lay down on my bed." Ben may be ninety-five years old but, as he says, "I still got all my marbles." He does, and I respect and trust him. So I did what he requested. After I lay down, he asked, "What do you see?"

"The ceiling? Your wall? The window?" I replied, feeling quite mystified. "Ben, I am not sure what I am supposed to see."

"See that wall?"

"Yes."

"All those certificates?"

The top half of the wall was covered with framed certificates and achievement awards Ben had been given over his lifetime. They represented a wide variety of areas in which he received recognition. For example, he had lived in Alaska before it became a state and was quite involved in the preservation of its natural resources. For recognition of his work in conservation, he received a coveted national award. He also had framed letters of commendation for his support of women's rights and had been made an honorary member of their organizations.

"Yes, I see them."

"My niece put them up there last week so I can look at them from the bed when I lie down. I was looking at them the other night, and I realized that I was not as worthless as I thought I was."

Two weeks earlier Ben had talked to me about how tough it was to get old and said he hoped he would die with dignity. At ninety-five, he was feeling worthless. Although I tried, nothing I said at the time could make him feel any differently.

I agree with Ben. God sure works in mysterious ways.

Walter

"My bags are packed!"

Those were the very first words Walter said to me when I walked into his room one day. Walter, however, is so weak that he can hardly sit upright in his wheelchair, let alone pack a suitcase.

Although Walter suffers from short-term memory loss, he is one of the most intelligent, articulate individuals I have ever had the privilege of meeting. At age ninety-two, he could hold his own with people half his age on any subject they would like to discuss. That is, when he is not dealing with pain beyond his threshold. The powerful drugs he is taking help, but at best, they control the pain only to a level that is tolerable.

Walter is well aware that his prognosis, as he says, "is not encouraging." Most of all he detests the thought of wasting away to nothing while not being able to enjoy any kind of quality of life. "When you know the person you have always been and, at the same time, realize what kind of existence you have ahead of you, it is too despairing to put into words," he says.

If you wonder what keeps Walter going, a mid-morning visit to his room would provide the answer. That is when he makes a phone call to his wife. "I call her every day," he says. "Have to tell her I love her."

His wife, though frail herself, still can get around well enough to live in the apartment they had shared before Walter's health required him to have more care than she and the family could provide. "This is the first time in our lives we have been separated," she says. Her daughter takes her to see Walter in the afternoon, but that morning phone call helps to begin the day for both of them.

"I love her," Walter says, "and I am concerned about her. If I died, it would be so hard on her. She is not so good herself; walks with a cane, had some major hip surgery a year ago. I wouldn't want to add to her problems."

As long as his wife is still living, Walter will do what he can to fight the prognosis. His bags, however, are packed.

Huddling

It was the coldest site in the cemetery, the funeral director said, and I certainly found no reason to disagree. We were on the top of a hill, with the wind blowing directly at us. The wind chill was estimated at thirty below. It was so cold that I could barely turn the pages in the service book, and since gloves would have hindered me, I had loaned mine to two of the pallbearers. One wore my left glove, the other, my right, as they both assisted in carrying the casket. They were grandsons who had flown in from warmer climates and were not prepared for the Arctic blast. Both had light jackets on, and neither had a hat. One of them, I believe, was even wearing sandals. The funeral director had the people huddle in a circle around me and the casket when we got to the grave. I felt more like a quarterback than a minister about to conduct a graveside service.

As I read the service I noticed the tears on the faces of many, including those grandsons, and I wondered how long it would take for a tear to freeze in that weather. Some might think that the tears were from eyes that watered because of the cold, but from talking to the family, I know differently.

There is a common assumption that when someone dies at a "ripe old age," the grief expressed is not so intense as that when someone younger dies. Yet one of the most intense grief situations I ever witnessed was at a visitation for an eighty-nine-year-old man. There had to be forty or more people in the room, and most of them were sobbing. He had been the mainstay of his family. They could comfort themselves by saying he had had a long life; nevertheless, because he was so deeply loved, it was hard for them to say good-bye.

It was no different that cold winter day on top of the hill. I will never forget the sight of those people huddling. When I reflect upon it, I think perhaps that is how family and friends should always gather at the grave. Huddled together tight, arms around each other, encircling the one they love.

George

George's wife, Gladys, is on the third floor of the Chronic Care section and has been there for the past two years. She is no longer able to communicate because of several strokes, and George wonders at times if Gladys recognizes him anymore as her husband. Each day George looks for any kind of familiar response that tells him this is still his wife sitting in this wheelchair. On good days Gladys opens her eyes and seems to have a smile for him. There may even be eye contact. The bad days, however, are beginning to outnumber the good. Nevertheless, George is faithful in his daily visiting with Gladys, taking her for a ride in her wheelchair, reading some of her favorite stories to her, feeding her during the noon meal, and sitting with her in chapel during services.

"Been married nearly fifty-two years," he says as he lovingly brushes back her hair and pats her gently on the cheek, hoping she'll open her eyes. "Even though Gladys is like this, she is still part of my life."

George is representative of so many who visit their spouses at the home. Upbeat and positive on the outside but so often grieving on the inside. They grieve over the fact that this is the first time they have really been separated from each other; they grieve over the relationship they once had but now see eroding due to things beyond their control. They will grieve the death when it comes, and, as strange as it sounds, they may also grieve losing the daily routine of coming to see their loved one. As to the latter, sometimes family members become volunteers because it would be too hard to lose not only their loved one but also the relationships they made with other residents and their families and with staff, all of whom they have come to know and love. There is comfort in staying connected with those who once knew their loved one.

George said something the other day that bears reflection by those of us who are trying to be supportive. We were talking about his situation and the anguish he feels as he watches his wife slip away from him a little every day.

"People say they understand what I am going through, and I believe they do," he says. Before going on, George pauses as he watches his wife fall asleep in her chair. They had been sitting together for the past hour. During that whole time, Gladys had not acknowledged in any way that he was even in the room. He sighs, looks out the window at the falling rain, and adds, "But there's a difference between understanding what I'm going through and feeling what I am feeling as I go through it."

Without response I think to myself, "Lord, I hope I know the difference."

Isabelle

When I first met Isabelle, she had just been moved into one of the double rooms in the Chronic Care section. Her boxes were being unpacked, and her family was beginning to put photographs up to make her half of the room more home-like. I wondered how she, at age ninety-six, would make the adjustment.

One of the most difficult times for anyone moving into a nursing home is the first day; in fact, the first few hours. They are entering into unfamiliar surroundings filled with unfamiliar faces. There are unfamiliar sights, unfamiliar sounds, and most of all, an unfamiliar bed. Many new residents will share with me that they are just overwhelmed. I remember one woman who refused to take off her coat. It was her way of protesting against all the changes going on around her. The decision to keep her coat on, I think, was one small thing she could do to retain some control. The staff understood and did not interfere. Another resident, a man in his eighties, told me the first day he moved in, "It felt like I was adrift on the ocean with no paddles."

It is certainly a time when family and friends are needed to help make the transition as easy as possible. One example that stands out in my mind is when five or six family members came with their father to make his first day easier. Some of them came early to prepare his new home. By the time he was wheeled into his room, the space had already been filled with some familiar belongings. He saw family pictures on one wall. On the other wall was a favorite painting he had always hung wherever he lived. The family stayed the whole day, sharing meals with him. At the dinner meal, a couple of his grandchildren showed up with "room warming" gifts.

Inasmuch as family members can be supportive and are very important in helping to make the transition a smooth one, often it simply comes down to the attitude of the resident. One ninety-three-year-old woman said, "I had to convince my family that I should be here. They didn't want to bring me. But I told them I wanted to come and that it was the right decision. It was."

Most of the residents who come in would admit that, if it were possible, they would rather be in their own homes. They realize, however, that life never stays the same. Knowing that from experience, they are determined to make the best of it and be positive.

Back to Isabelle. When I entered her room that day to introduce myself, I wondered what her attitude would be about the move. She was sitting in her wheelchair, a lap robe on, quietly watching the family unpack her boxes. As we chatted, I discovered Isabelle to have a warm, positive outlook upon life. Her family was important and so was her faith. It was her response to something I said that told me she had the kind of attitude that would help in making the transition to her new home. I had knelt down in front of her so that we would have eye contact and said after we had chatted for awhile, "Isabelle, I think I am going to like you."

Smiling, and with a twinkle in her eyes, she replied, "You are supposed to love me."

Ruby

Having finished their coffee and cookies, the dozen or so residents were settling in for the Bible study. The subject for discussion was how to handle disputes. As an opening question, I asked, "If you were having a dispute with another resident, how would you go about settling it?"

Ruby, who is barely five feet tall and weighs probably around ninety pounds, crinkled up her nose, raised her arm above her head, shook a clenched fist, and announced to all, "I would bop them in the nose!"

When I think of what the residents, in their circumstances, have to deal with, I am surprised there are not a number of "bopped noses." Many people comment about how difficult it is when two people get married and have to adjust to having another person around all the time. Can you imagine living with 400 other people all the time? It is true there are those who have private rooms and thus have their own space. But as one resident who does have a private room remarked, "As soon as you walk out your door, you meet people you know and who want to strike up a conversation. Mealtimes are always shared with three other people at the table. You can't get away from people unless you shut yourself up in your room, but who wants to do that? Then you become a prisoner in your own room." The person who shared these words is an outgoing person who likes people but just needs her own space and some privacy from time to time.

Those in Chronic Care have even less privacy, for they must share a room, due to cost considerations. Imagine sharing a space that is about the size of an average bedroom and also serves as living quarters. Imagine two hard-of-hearing people, each watching a personal TV in the same small room. Or one person having classical music on one radio while another listens to country western on another. Imagine sharing a small bathroom. Or trying to sleep when your roommate has a light on. Or....

Bopped noses? Amazingly, I have not seen one yet. I wonder why.

Ivah

Ivah will tell you that she feels like a freak at times.

Ivah is an attractive woman and had always been complimented on her beautiful smile, but she makes no attempt to smile these days. She is recovering from a series of strokes, and one side of her body is paralyzed. When someone tries to bring a smile, she simply turns her head and looks away. Staff will tell you that it is very hard to get her to use a mirror to groom herself.

Through therapy Ivah is regaining some of her speech, but it is a very slow process. Though she knows what she wants to say, she is unable to find the words to express herself, and the frustration shows. No one needs to tell her that she slurs her words and that one side of her mouth droops. Sometimes she will bring up her hand to cover that part of her mouth as she tries to speak. She works hard in speech therapy, even though she knows that the prognosis is not good. Her only hope is to regain partial control of her ability to speak so that she can be more clearly understood. She knows she will never regain the use of her right arm. And, for her, the beautiful smile she was always complimented on is now just a memory.

Mealtimes have been difficult for Ivah. Having been right-handed, she is now learning to eat with her left—not an easy task for someone who has been using the other hand for over eighty years. As she looks at her right hand lying helplessly in her lap, she will tell you that it is like losing an old friend.

Detesting the bib she wears, Ivah reluctantly allows it to be placed around her neck. Her new "good" hand is quite unsteady as she tries to feed herself. She says that it all seems backwards. Though help would be there for the asking, she is determined to maintain a degree of dignity and tries to do as much for herself as she can. Within a short time, however, her dignity, along with the bib, is soiled with orange Jell-O. Perhaps if she were eighty years younger, one might smile and take a picture.

During the meal, Ivah accidentally tips over her glass of milk. In an effort to clean it up, she only makes it worse. As fate would have it, someone walks by at just that moment; unfortunately, it is a first-time visitor to the facility. He looks at the soiled orange bib, the milk now spilling onto her lap, and says in a tone that is as controlled as his smile, "I'll get someone to help."

Ivah looks up and replies, "Ah... napkins... ah... milk... ah...."

"Don't worry, I will get someone," he says quickly, looking around for staff. His words seem friendly and calm, but his face registers ever so slightly a look Ivah has seen before. Finally, a staff person comes and the man leaves. Only when he reaches the door leading out of the dining room does he glance back.

"We'll take care of this," the aide says to Ivah. "Don't you worry."

"I... ah... feel... ah... ah... like... freak."

Soulmates

Hildur isn't a nursing home resident, but her faith and strength of character in the face of difficult circumstances would have made her a soulmate to Mildred, who was.

First, let me tell you about Hildur. She was a member of a small country church I served many years ago. Hildur, eighty-seven years old, was considered a "shut-in"; that is, she was not physically able to come to church. Members of the church would visit her, and I would bring her communion on a regular basis. Hildur had not taken a step out of her house for years, yet she was widely known and respected throughout the community. Whenever friends were going through difficult times, she would write them a note to let them know that she was keeping them in her prayers. She often wrote and prayed from her bed. She said once, "My bed is my altar."

The notes would not be long, maybe a short paragraph or two, sometimes only two or three sentences. The power of her notes, however, was not in how much she wrote but in the fact that she wrote them at all. Hildur had such a serious heart condition that it would take her two hours to get dressed in the morning. She told me that writing a note or two and having prayers for the person took so much out of her, she would have to lie down for a long time. Those who received her notes were deeply touched because they knew the price Hildur paid for writing them. To suggest that perhaps she should stop writing the notes for her own well-being would be like telling her to stop breathing.

Mildred was a resident who could have been Hildur's soulmate. During the time she was at the home, Mildred was so weakened by her physical condition that she was bedridden. She was also in constant pain, but she never complained. Her attitude was that through faith, she could learn from her pain. When we talked about what she was going through, she told me she knew God did not cause the pain. She did not believe she was being tested or punished. She understood and accepted that her ninety-two-year-old body was just plain running down. My visits with her were short because of her labored breathing. As weak as she was, however, she would still write notes to family and friends, as a way of keeping them in her prayers. She once said something that told me that she and Hildur could have been soulmates. When asked about the energy it took to write those notes, she smiled and said, "My prayers are in my pen."

If you should ever receive a note from someone like Hildur or Mildred, treasure it, for more than likely, it was quite costly to write.

Being a Parent

Her son died nearly twelve years ago. "I still can feel the touch of his hand upon my arm," Edith says, her eyes moistening with tears. "He was only fifty-nine years old."

Although Edith is ninety-three years old, the memory of sitting next to her son's hospital bed is as vivid to her today as the reality was then. "There isn't a day that goes by that I don't think about him," she says, as she looks around for a tissue. "Such a good man. He was too young to have that terrible heart attack." After wiping her eyes, she looks at her son's picture on her dresser.

People tell me that of all the heartaches that the years may bring, none is as painful as outliving one's children.

John, another resident, points to his son's photograph on the wall. It is a picture of a young man smiling proudly. He is wearing an army uniform. "I miss him," John says as he touches his chest. "I have this ache in my heart. It never goes away."

His son was killed in World War Two. He was only nineteen at the time and had enlisted just two months earlier. Although it happened over fifty years ago, John still deeply feels the loss. He says slowly, in a voice quivering with emotion, "I will always hurt for my son until the day I die." He pauses and adds, "I hope to see him again."

The saying, "You never cease to be a parent," may be a cliché, but it is one that has stood the test of the years in life and in death. Just ask Edith and John.

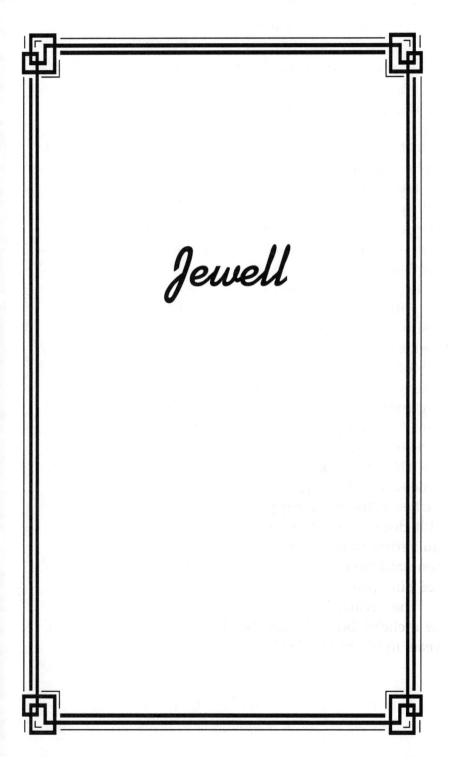

Jewell

The other day I saw Mickey Mouse in a wheelchair. Actually, Mickey was not *in* the chair. He was hovering above it, floating in the air, bobbing up and down as the string attached to the helium-filled balloon with Mickey's smiling face was being gently tugged by Jewell who occupied the chair. The balloon, bearing the words *Happy Birthday*, had been tied to Jewell's wheelchair by a family member earlier that day. When I told Jewell that he and Mickey were born on the same day (I had heard on the radio that it was the 50th anniversary of the birth of the famous mouse), Jewell laughed and then quipped, "But I was born first."

Although Jewell has spent the last five years in a wheelchair, he continues to display a sharp wit and a keen sense of humor concerning his circumstances. Now, in his late 70s, he's been a resident at the nursing home for nearly seven years. Very seldom do you see him without a smile. Jewell is a man determined not to let life get him down; he is always joking with the staff about one thing or another. For example, on those Sundays when he decides to stay for both chapel services, he will say with a grin, "Chaplain, I need a double dose today." As further evidence of his playful approach to life, I once overheard Jewell telling a new volunteer who was passing out cookies and coffee that it was his birthday. After congratulating Jewell, she gave him an extra cookie. "For your birthday," she said. After she walked away, I went up to Jewell and asked, "Didn't I hear you tell someone yesterday that it was your birthday? And the day before that as well?" He just winked at me as he took another bite of his cookie.

One might assume that Jewell is one of those elderly people who don't have a care in the world, and that he is spending his last days enjoying life the best he can. That is true to a certain extent, but there is another side of him that needs to be shared.

Jewell served in the Navy during World War Two and on more than one of our visits together, he shared with me some of his experiences. At first, he talked about the training he and his friends went through and the ship they were assigned. During our last visit, though, he talked about his friends who were killed in action. As he spoke, tears formed in his eyes and his voice cracked with emotion.

"They were such good men," he said. "And they were so young."

His voice dropped to a whisper as he continued. "They're never far from me." Jewell wet his lips and swallowed hard. "You know, I've thought about those guys just about every day for the past fifty years." He paused, looked at me with his pale blue eyes, and then said with a knowing half-smile, "Soon I'll be joining them."

Neither one of us said anything for a long time. We understood that our silence was a way of honoring those who had died.

"They were such good men." Jewell repeated the words as if he were pronouncing a benediction.

"You miss them, don't you?"

Jewell did not immediately respond. He looked away for a moment, shifted in his wheelchair, and then replied, "Yeah, I do. I should have been with them. I don't know why I was spared."

We talked further about his friends who died in action. Jewell described them in such a way that I felt I also knew them. There was Jack, who was planning to go into his father's hardware business after the war;

Ralph, whose girlfriend wrote twice a day; Skip, who was the joker of the group. "I close my eyes at night," Jewell told me, "and I can see their faces. I'll never...." His voice cracked with emotion again, and he cleared his throat. "I'll never forget them and all the others."

For Jewell, remembering his friends and others who were killed during the war is a given; it is done without question. Memorial Day is more than just a holiday to Jewell. It is sacred, and he wonders if the younger generation fully understands and appreciates its significance.

If you should ever visit a nursing home and see a wheelchair with a Mickey Mouse balloon bopping above it, take a moment to walk over and say hello to the man who is sitting in the chair and tugging on the string. After you do, you might also want to say thanks and then share a moment of silence in memory of those who died so young.

Ellen

If you were to visit Ellen on any day of the week, you would probably find her sitting and quietly talking to a teddy bear she cradles in her arms. The bear has only one eye, a nose that has been repaired a number of times, a head with hardly any fur on top, and stuffing coming out of one leg. Certainly not in the best condition, but the bear will probably outlast Ellen.

Some might look upon the two of them and feel only pity. "What a pair," they would say. "That bear probably is less confused than she is." Others could take a different attitude. I overheard one person remark, "Isn't it pathetic? Imagine, a grown woman holding on to a stuffed animal for God-knows-what reason." And, of course, there would always be a few who would snicker, "Did you see that poor woman? The one in the wheelchair?"

I asked Ellen one day, "Who are you holding?"

"Oh," she replied, smiling, "a friend."

Her friend comes to Bible study and chapel services with her. The teddy bear is with her when she laughs at something funny, listens to her as she repeats the same stories about her late husband day after day, lets her cry when she feels bad or lonely without trying to fix it. He does not look at her strangely when she thinks she is still living at home with her mother. He sits with her hours upon end as she looks out the window at nothing in particular and is always ready to be hugged, squeezed, kissed, and patted on the head. He puts up with her bad moods and does not leave her when she is sick. Her friend accepts her for who she is, is there for her in the morning and when she goes to bed at night, and will be with her when she dies.

Imagine, a grown woman holding on to a stuffed animal for God-knows-what reason.

August

August Henry Svienski is his full name, and he likes to be known around the nursing home as a mean, ornery old cuss.

When you get to know August, however, you find that he is more of a *lovable*, mean, ornery old cuss. To say that he is a character is an understatement—he *is* a character. He is one of several ventriloquist figures I use in my work as a chaplain.

How the mean old cuss got his name is a story in itself. We had a contest among the residents to name him when he first came to "live" at the nursing home. More than twenty-five residents submitted names. "It was my grandfather's name," said Hilda, the winner of the contest. As the winner, she received an 8 1/2" x 11" framed photograph of August. He even autographed it for her. She has the picture hanging on the wall in her room.

"I tell everybody that it's a picture of my first husband," Hilda says, and then adds with a chuckle, "I even had the doctor fooled one day. He had to get up real close to examine the picture. I sure got a good laugh out of that one."

August may not be a *real* person, but don't try telling that to Hilda and the other residents. They accept him as one of them.

"He's so ugly, he's cute," said Bertha, an 83-year old resident, as she watched August knot his bushy-white eyebrows, wrinkle his brow, and twitch his big, hooked nose. He doesn't say much, but when he does, watch out. His voice sounds like a load of gravel being dumped on cement. His tone of voice may be gruff, but he has a way of flirting with the ladies—and they love it. His bib overalls, plaid flannel shirt, and cowboy boots add to his charm and personality.

One reason August is so well-liked by the residents is that when it comes to getting old, he tells it like it is. Once, when August was visiting with a group of residents, one of them asked him how he was doing. August screwed up his eyes and grumbled, "Terrible. Got this arthritis in my knees." A number of the residents shook their heads in agreement, acknowledging that they had aches and pains from arthritis as well.

"August," Claire asked, "how do your knees feel?"

"How do you think they feel," August snapped. "They hurt like hell!"

The reaction of the residents to August's candor was tittering laughter and the nodding of heads in agreement. August had spoken for them. And I can just imagine what some of them could have been thinking in terms of how they might respond the next time a nurse asks them how their arthritis is doing.

Another example of August's lovable candor surfaced when he was visiting residents in the dining room during their noon meal. As a staff person was serving coffee to a table of four women, one of them asked, "August, what would you like to drink?" Without missing a beat, August looked up at the nurse and growled, "I'll have a beer." No sooner had he said that, than Sylvia, a petite woman well into her 90s piped up, "Oh, that sounds good to me, too."

August visits with the residents and talks to them about the aches and pains that come with growing old; he jokes with them about the aging process; and he speaks frankly about death and dying. They love him because he understands their feelings and expresses their unspoken thoughts. And when I don't bring him around, they ask about him, and tell me to say hello to him for them.

This may sound strange, but I think we all could learn a lot from August in terms of relating to older people. I know I have.

Roscoe
and
Wallace

Roscoe and Wallace came out of the chapel one Sunday morning with arms locked, helping each other to use canes for balance. Their gait was unsteady but they were determined to help each other make it back to their rooms. It was heartwarming to watch and listen to these two joke and laugh about what they were doing.

I suppose it is not uncommon to see people helping each other, but in a setting such as ours, and because of the age and physical condition of the individuals, the act takes on an added dimension. The circumstances in which these acts of kindness take place are oftentimes incredible. Consider, for instance, this example. One day while walking through the North Wing of the Alzheimer's Unit, I heard one of the residents yelling, "Help, help." Since those in this wing are in the advanced stages of the disease, yelling for help could be anything from a resident hallucinating to simply repeating the words throughout the day. It's not uncommon for residents to cry out for assistance, and when staff come and ask what they need, no answer is given.

In this case, the cry for help came from an activity room in which there were a half dozen or more residents. Most of them were in wheelchairs, either asleep or staring off into space. A few were in rockers, looking out the window. None were paying any attention to the person who was yelling.

The shouts were coming from Orrin, a man who normally mumbles a few words every now and then as he sits in his wheelchair. In the six months he has been here, I have not heard a complete sentence from him, and what he does say is usually not very clear. He was still yelling, "Help, help," when I walked in and asked him what was wrong. I did not expect to get any kind of response that I could understand. Orrin's head moved to his right and bent downward. When I looked at where I thought he was looking, I saw a pair of glasses belonging to a woman nearby. They had fallen to the floor and she could not reach them because of being in her wheelchair. I picked them up and helped her put them on. Then I turned to Orrin and said, "Orrin, is this what you were yelling 'Help' about?" The only response I got was a slight smile. Though Orrin had needs of his own, he received satisfaction from helping another.

Getting back to Roscoe and Wallace. I need to tell you what they were really laughing and joking about as they helped guide each other back to their rooms from chapel. Wallace had commented to his friend, "This is like the blind leading the blind."

What is so remarkable about Wallace's comment is that it was literally true. You see, both he and Roscoe are legally blind.

Two Nurses

I was at an all-day conference when I got the message. It came from the Transitional Care Unit, a twenty-bed wing that handles patients who are released from hospitals but who are not able to fully care for themselves at home. The focus in the unit is on physical therapy and rehabilitation. The average length of stay is fifteen days. The TCU staff called that day for the chaplain because they felt that a certain patient who had developed congestive heart failure would not last much longer. Fortunately, I was within ten minutes of the facility. The family had been called and would be there within the half hour.

When I got to the room, a nurse was just finishing checking on the patient and making sure she was comfortable. Having acknowledged my presence, the nurse left, quietly closing the door. I sat in a chair next to the bed, spoke the woman's name and introduced myself. Her eyes remained closed, and she made no indication that she knew I was present. In such situations, however, when the person appears to be unresponsive, I always speak to them as if they do hear what I am saying. I encourage families to do the same.

I read some scripture aloud and then had a short prayer, closing with the words, "Lord, let thy servant depart in peace." Within a short time, no longer than a minute or two, she took her last breath and died.

I sat there for a couple of minutes, collecting my thoughts, feeling the sacredness of the moment. It is a special privilege to be present at the moment of death. Other staff have said this as well. It doesn't always happen as peacefully as this, but this time it did, and I was thankful that I could share it with the family, for I knew they would be comforted by the manner in which she died.

Noting the time of death, I went to inform the nurses and then went back to the room. When the two nurses who had been caring for the woman came in, I asked if I could be of any help. They thanked me but said it was not necessary. I watched them as they removed the oxygen tube, smoothed her hair and gently covered her arms with the blanket. They were professional, and they did their job in a loving, caring way. When I asked them how they were doing, I discovered the depth of their caring. They started crying, and one, speaking for both of them, said it was so hard because when you care for people day after day, you get to really know them. We hugged and then had a prayer together as we stood by the bedside. When I left the room they were continuing to do the things they needed to do, but with tears in their eyes.

As I write this, I am reminded of the story about the one-time Speaker of the House, Sam Rayburn. When, near the end of his life, he discovered just how ill he was, he surprised his colleagues in Congress by announcing that he was going home to Bonham, Texas. "Why, though?" they asked. "Why go to such a not-even-on-the-map kind of place for medical tests and treatment when the best medical facilities in the world are available to you in Washington, D.C. and on the East Coast?" Rayburn told them why: "Bonham, Texas is a place where people know it when you are sick and care when you die."

One day two nurses, who are representative of many professional caregivers, made it possible for me to say to a family that their mother died peacefully among people who cared.

Hector

No sooner had I offered the blessing for the noon meal than a staff person came over to me, snickering. She was eager to relate the experience she had with Hector just before the prayer. She had just put his plate down when he snarled at her, "Damn it! I don't want gravy." The next words they both heard were those of the prayer: "We thank you for the staff who care for us, for their patience and understanding, especially at those times when we are not very nice to be around. Bless them and bless this food. Amen."

Contrary to what some may think, Hector has always been a very quiet, gentle man. Now in his eighties, however, he is beginning to show signs of dementia. His outburst may have been uncharacteristic of Hector and who he had always been but not uncharacteristic of what happens with persons suffering from dementia. As you may know, dementia means a loss or impairment of mental powers. It refers to the symptoms that appear when various parts of the brain are damaged. Symptoms include changes such as confusion, disorientation, memory loss, irritability, and other aspects of mental malfunction.

Family members are often embarrassed by outbursts from their loved one using language that might make a Marine Corps drill instructor blush. One family told me, with tears of anguish, that they just could not understand where their very religious mother learned the words that were coming forth from her now. It is important for family and friends to understand that brain cell damage results in problems that the person cannot control or prevent. As Hector's dementia increases, more than likely, so will his outbursts.

The staff person Hector scolded certainly was not offended by his outburst. She and other staff are often the target of such flare-ups. It happens daily. They take the occurrences in stride, however, because they understand the nature of the disease. And, of course, the staff person's snickering was not aimed at Hector but was simply her way of finding humor in what could have been a difficult situation.

And what about Hector? As I passed his table, he smiled and thanked me for the nice prayer. As he settled down to have a quiet meal, he did not remember his outburst or the language he had used. To the staff, even if his outbursts increase, Hector will always be thought of as a nice, decent man.

Anna

It never fails. Whenever I announce that a nursing home resident has died, Anna always motions for me to come over to her and she asks, "What I want to know is, who is the person that died?"

It is not that Anna is so hard of hearing, nor is it because she is nosy and simply needs to know everything. The truth of the matter is, she cares.

Certainly, when a death occurs on her floor, it is upsetting because Anna knows the person. But it is also upsetting to her when the death occurs in another part of the facility. She wants to be sure to know the name, even if she has never met the person. There are no impersonal deaths where Anna is concerned, and she is not alone in showing this compassion.

A nursing home is one of the most caring communities I have ever encountered in all my years of ministry. I am not talking simply about the staff being caregivers to the residents. The residents also give care to staff and to one another. I can feel the compassion and concern being shown as I watch one resident in a wheelchair helping push another. Or listen as a resident explains to a visually-impaired tablemate where the portions of food are on the plate. It becomes especially poignant when you know that the resident doing the explaining is partially paralyzed on one side because of a stroke she had two years ago. Along this same thought, I remember Elizabeth, who was given a chance to move to another floor to be with more independent people. She declined. Her reason was that she felt it important to stay where she was because the woman who shared her room was quite confused and needed her help. Elizabeth would not leave her friend.

As I write these thoughts, another resident comes to mind. I have witnessed Clarence's compassion. He seems to have the gift of discerning the feelings of others. On one occasion, he went to someone who was crying, taking her a box of tissues. Another time, though he was sitting in a chair halfway down the hall, I watched him struggle to get up to go sit with another resident, who was despondent. He just seemed to sense that the person needed some company. Sitting down next to him, Clarence put his hand on the man's shoulder and gently patted it. He could not offer any words of comfort. You see, due to his Alzheimer's, he no longer had verbal communication skills.

As I mentioned, residents also extend their care to the staff. When residents learn of a certain staff member going through difficult times, such as a death in the family or an illness, they share their concern with cards, prayers, and verbal expressions of support and encouragement. They can be very affirming of a staff member as an individual who does so much for them. Staff frequently will say that one of the benefits of working in such a community is the love and nurturing they receive from those they care for.

Certainly, you will find suffering and death in a nursing home. But with a closer look, you will find a community of truly caring, compassionate people like Anna who want to make sure they always know the name of the person who died.

Estelle and Leo

"Thank you, Chaplain, for holding my hand," Estelle said in a voice barely above a whisper.

I'd just gotten up from the chair next to Estelle's bed, and I had to bend down to hear her. She had not been doing well for the past several days, and her daughter had asked me to stop in to see her. Now in her late 80s, Estelle had recently been diagnosed with cancer. While the doctors were concerned about the cancer and how they would treat it, they were especially worried about a heart condition that left her so weak that at times she could barely lift her arms. When I first walked into Estelle's room, I could tell by the look on her face that she was troubled. I assumed (wrongly) that it was the cancer diagnosis that was the cause of her anxiety.

"Hi, Estelle, how're you doing?" I said.

"Oh, Chaplain, my daughter won't be here until this evening. That's so far away. I wish she were here now."

"She's a great comfort to you, isn't she?"

"Oh, yes. And if she was here right now, do you know what she would be doing?"

"No, I don't."

Estelle closed her eyes for a moment and then sighed. "She'd be holding my hand."

"Well, I'm not your daughter, but will I do?" I asked.

Estelle smiled and moved her hand ever so slightly toward me. For the next fifteen minutes we talked about a number of things concerning her health and how she felt about what was happening to her. I discovered that she was not overly concerned about the cancer or her heart condition.

"This old body is just plain running down," she said. "I never thought I'd live this long, anyway. All my brothers and sisters have died. I'm the last one left."

As I was about to leave, she thanked me, and I knew that for her the most important thing I had done was to hold her hand. She did not expect me to cure her cancer or fix her damaged heart. She was thankful for the touching of our hands. And so was I.

As a chaplain I find myself holding the hands of many residents, both men and women. The circumstances always vary: Bob, who was just informed about the death of his 60-year-old son; Betty, who is depressed over the loss of her eyesight due to glaucoma; Claire, who can barely stand the daily pain of her arthritis and prays that God will take her home to heaven; Sanford, who is very fearful of using a wheelchair for the rest of his life because his hip replacement is not healing as well as it should.

I recall Leo, a gregarious man who, unfortunately, is in the beginning stages of Alzheimer's. Leo and I were sitting next to each other in a spacious room used for large gatherings. In attendance that afternoon were nearly 150 residents and staff members. We were there listening to a band that had come to play the dance tunes of the 1940s. The music of Glenn Miller and Jimmy Dorsey filled the air. It was a party-like atmosphere. Refreshments were served, and a portable dance floor had been set up. Volunteers were going around asking residents if they would like to dance.

"Leo, did you dance when you were younger?" I asked. I had noticed him tapping his foot to the beat of the music.

"Oh, yes. I loved to dance." He looked out at those dancing and then back to me, "I was a good dancer, too," Leo said proudly. "They're good, but I was better."

"Are you going to get out there now and dance?" I asked him.

Leo looked at me, smiled slightly, and shook his head. "Oh, no, my old legs couldn't take it."

Leo and I continued to listen to the music as we watched the people dance. I could only imagine what was going through his mind. I wondered what kind of memories were being brought forth. Before long, Leo put his hand on mine. "Why do we have to get old?" he asked. The look in his eyes reflected the sadness in his voice.

"That's a good question." I paused as I thought about a nurse who shared with me the best answer she ever heard to the question Leo had just asked. She said she overheard two elderly residents talking about why people have to get old and die. One of them answered, "Because we've got to get off the planet to make room for all the new ones." I considered sharing that comment with Leo but instead replied, "Leo, I gotta think about that."

As we sat there, I wondered how I could answer Leo's question. From a scientific perspective? A gerontological perspective? Perhaps a theological perspective? I decided that none of those approaches would be appropriate, and that they could not provide an adequate answer. "I don't know the answer," I said. "I wish I did."

I took Leo's hand in mine and as I did, he squeezed my hand, and I, his. In that moment, we were simply two human beings pondering one of the mysteries of life. Leo and I, as was the case with myself and Estelle, were bonded by the touch of our hands.

Family and friends so often express feelings of frustration when they visit an elderly loved one. As one woman said to me about her 98-year-old aunt, "I don't know what I can do anymore. I can't bring her books to read because her eyesight is so poor. We can't carry on a decent conversation because her hearing is so bad. She complains about her pains and I can't do anything about them. I feel so helpless."

"You can always hold her hand," I told her.

"But isn't there any more I can do?" she asked.

Thinking about Estelle and Leo, I replied, "Sometimes that's the most important thing in the world you can do."

Wilbur

Wilbur always says about his life, "I should write a book." But he won't.

Like so many elderly nursing home residents, Wilbur has fascinating stories to share. He remembers sitting on his grandfather's lap and being told the tale of when, as a young lad, his grandfather marched as a drummer boy in the Civil War. Still having a vivid picture of the man on whose lap he sat, Wilbur remembers the white beard reaching down to his grandfather's knees. Then there was the story about another relative who had an audience with President Abraham Lincoln. Wilbur, himself, was a blacksmith as a young adult and had many interesting stories to tell from that work experience.

When you hear the stories the elderly share, it is like listening to talking history books. One resident told me what it was like to fight in the Battle of the Bulge during World War Two. Another shared that she really did not lead a very exciting life, but she thought maybe I would like to hear the story of her once having tea with Eleanor Roosevelt at the White House. Still another shared some great stories of when she led an "all-girl traveling band." Memories of the Depression, the first flush toilets, when nylons first became popular, having Harry Houdini as a next door neighbor, and so on. Each resident could write a book.

Some families are writing down stories or recording them on tape so they are not lost. What a treasure they will be to not only the current generation but the next as well. Imagine what priceless gifts these stories on tape will be, to be presented like family heirlooms and passed down through the generations.

Take this storytelling even a step further. Why not use the elderly as a resource in teaching our young people? Imagine setting up a series of interviews with the elderly so that students can experience history come alive. Perhaps an experimental classroom could be set up in a nursing home setting. Why not allow those who have lived history to make a contribution to the education of the next generation? Why not have a computer program set up so that the picture and voice of the person come across on the screen, telling a story about what it was like when indoor plumbing became a reality or what a blacksmith's job was all about?

If you are looking around for a good story, I think I can help you. I know where there are a number of great stories that may not have been written yet but are just waiting to be told.

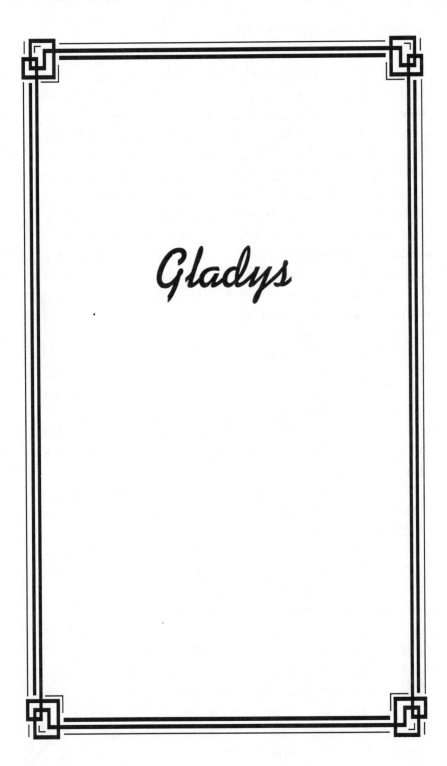

Gladys

Gladys liked it when I called her a "tough old cookie." She took it as a compliment, and it was meant to be one. The next day she came to my office to share a story about her mother and how tough a cookie she was. It seemed that a neighbor had come to visit her mother one morning after her father had gone to town. This neighbor, who had a reputation of taking advantage of a situation when he thought he could get away with it, made a pass at Gladys' mother. When I asked Gladys what happened, she first had to describe her mother. "She was a little woman, not much taller than five feet, and I doubt if she weighed a hundred pounds. Do you get the picture?"

"Yes, I think I do. She was a pretty small lady."

Gladys nodded approvingly. "Well, no sooner had the words come out of that man's mouth," she chuckled, "than my mother decked him. He never bothered her again." Having told her story, Gladys got up and left. She didn't have to say it, but we both knew why she told me that story. She had come from a long line of tough cookies.

There are quite a number of tough cookies who reside in nursing homes. Anyone spending time in one of these facilities could not help but notice the residents' daily acts of courage. Just getting up in the morning, knowing that you have a day of aches and pains ahead of you, can be an act of courage. Gladys, for example, has to contend with painful joints every waking moment. Then, for Gladys and others like her, there is the trip to P.T. a couple times a week. We think those initials stand for *Physical Therapy*. The residents, however, will tell you that the letters really stand for *Physical Torture*. They know they have to go through it for their own benefit, but that doesn't make it any easier. Viewing it all with a sense of humor makes it more bearable.

One of the favorite sayings of the residents is, "Growing old is not for sissies!" People like Gladys will explain how much energy it takes to deal with pain that never goes away. The constant pain makes them feel tired, and they have to push themselves to do even the simplest tasks. "It takes energy even to tell people about the pain," one resident said, adding, "Sometimes, to save energy, I would just say I was doing okay even though I was not. Besides, my family doesn't need to hear all of it. They have enough worries of their own." There are many residents who deal with pain day after day and still get up to face it again the next day. In anybody's book, that qualifies for a "tough cookie" award.

The faith of these people is even more remarkable in that it has stood the spiritual trials and tribulations that come with the aging process. It doesn't mean they never have questions such as, Why isn't God taking me home? or Why am I still around when I am like this? or Why do I have to suffer so? Their faith isn't questionable, but they do have a questioning faith.

Each of us no doubt could think of people whose names are well-known and who could be thought of as spiritual heroes of our day and age. There are, however, those not-so-famous people who also could serve as role models people like Mildred and Ebert and Louise and Frank and, of course, Gladys. These and others like them are examples of courage as they face the daily struggles that come with the aging process. There are many examples to draw upon from those who live within our long-term care facilities. To fail to see and hear their testimony of faith is not only to do a disservice to them, but also to ourselves.

Gladys and countless others like her show that there are some pretty tough cookies around. If you are looking for role models of strength and courage and faith, you just may find them in what many might consider to be the most unlikely of places.

Before you go to visit that relative or friend in a nursing home, consider these questions: What really constitutes courage and faith in a human being? Is it possible to be confined to a wheelchair or a bed and still be a role model? And how many tough cookies have you known in your lifetime?

Merle

Merle, "the old story teller" offered to share a cookie with me the other day. He and his daughter appeared at the open door to my office. They had just returned from having coffee and cookies, and he had two cookies left.

"You can have one if you'd like," he said. He held out a plastic bag containing the cookies. "They're homemade. My daughter here baked them."

"No, thank you, but I'll take one of your stories," I said. That brought a smile to Merle's face. He motioned to his daughter to wheel his wheelchair into my office. I pulled up a chair next to him, sat down, and got comfortable as I looked forward to hearing him spin one of his yarns. His daughter, obviously proud of her father's storytelling, stood behind the wheelchair, her hand on his thin shoulder. She was pleased that there was this opportunity, because she knew (as I did) that her father loved telling stories. Merle has gained such a reputation for his storytelling among the staff members and residents that his daughter put a sign outside his room that reads, in big, bold letters—"The Old Storyteller."

"It happened back in the 1930s." Merle began. He spoke softly so I pulled my chair closer. "I was just a young man at the time," he continued. "Don't exactly remember how old I was, but I must of been 18 or 19. Me and my friend decided to ride our motorcycles out to the Black Hills of South Dakota."

"Merle, that's a pretty long ride on a motorcycle," I said.

"Sure is, and back then the roads weren't all that good," Merle replied. He paused, looking straight ahead in a daze, as if he were being taken back by his memories. I wondered if he was back on his motorcycle, looking at the road ahead of him. After a while, he turned toward me.

"We made it, though, and had a few experiences along the way. It was a pretty interesting trip."

"I bet it was, Merle," I said. "What do you remember most about the trip?"

"Heh, heh, that's easy. It was when my friend accidentally shot himself in the leg. We had to flag down a car to get him to the hospital. And you know what, now that I come to think of it?"

"What's that?" I asked.

"The driver of that car was a preacher." The old storyteller chuckled. "Anyway, we got my friend some medical help. Doc said he was lucky. It wasn't a serious wound, but it taught him to be careful with guns."

"Well, how did it happen?" I wondered.

"My friend don't remember for sure. I guess he was just holding the gun and it went off. We finished the rest of the trip, though."

"That's a great story," I told him. "Do you have any more stories to tell?"

Merle's eyes twinkled as he grinned. "Sure, got lots of them, but you're going to have to get a shovel if I tell them all."

Each time Merle and I meet, he has another story to share. A couple of days after I had heard the story of the motorcycle trip, I saw Merle in the hallway. He was sitting in his wheelchair, watching people walk by. For a moment, I pictured him as a young man sitting on a motorcycle and revving up the engine.

"Hello there, you old storyteller," I said. I squatted down so that we would have eye contact. "Have you got a story for me today?"

Merle grinned and rubbed his chin. "Sure do."

"Great. Let's hear it."

"Back home one winter it was so cold, the creek behind the house froze. I got out and cleaned off a patch so that we (I learned later that the *we* referred to Merle and his wife, whom he called Momma in the story) could go ice-skating. This was over thirty years ago. I don't think that creek has been frozen since. Anyway, Momma and I went skating."

"How often did the two of you go skating?" I asked.

"Never before. That was the first time Momma had been on skates in all our years of marriage. She had brand new skates on. Me, I had on my old skates. I'd used them for them years. They worked pretty good. Didn't need new ones."

Merle scratched his chin before going on. "Anyway, Momma started to twirl around, and when I reached out for her, we both went down. Ker-plunk! She broke her arm."

"Oh, no," I said in a half-whisper.

"Yep."

"What happened then?" I asked.

The old storyteller winked at me and chuckled. "That was the last time we put on skates. I hung up my skates right next to hers."

"Merle, what a wonderful story, " I said.

"I've got another one for you next time, too," he assured me.

"Good, I'll look forward to it."

Merle's storytelling is important because his stories invite others to see him from a different perspective. When you hear his stories, he is no longer an elderly nursing home resident in a wheelchair. He becomes an adventurous young man traveling across the country on a motorcycle; or a husband sweeping snow from a frozen creek so that he and his wife can form yet another memory, even if it's a memory of a broken arm and a pair of well-used skates hanging next to a pair of skates that were used only once.

Theodore

It was the most solemn moment in the Mass. Those who had come for the service in the chapel sat in reverent anticipation. They watched silently as the young priest who was officiating consecrated the elements. He was about to drink the wine in the chalice. Having made the sign of the cross, the priest raised the cup to his lips when Theodore yelled out in a voice loud enough to be heard by all in attendance, "Jesus Christ! Is he going to drink that whole damned thing?"

Theodore's comment may sound humorous to some and, I dare say, blasphemous to others. To Theodore, however, it was a serious question, asked without malice. He was not trying to be sarcastic or funny. Like many people with the disease of Alzheimer's, Theodore's feelings and thoughts are often unashamedly expressed.

When you are dealing with victims of Alzheimer's, you usually know what they are feeling at any given moment. If they are happy with you, they'll smile and may even take your hand. They are certainly not shy about saying the things that are on their minds. Albert, for example, saw nothing wrong (or politically incorrect) in telling a young nursing aide that she was beautiful and had shapely legs. "I'd like to date you if I was younger," he told her. In the same vein, Christina saw nothing wrong in flirting with me—and she understood that I was the chaplain. "You're cute," she said as she took my arm to walk down to the room where we were going to have a worship service. After the service, she would often go out and sit on the couch with Milton, her "boyfriend." The two of them could be seen holding hands. Occasionally, when they were in one or the other's room, the staff would have to gently remind them to keep the door open. Christina has been married for more than sixty years but, because of Alzheimer's, she has not recognized her husband for the past seven months. She seems to know him and says, "Oh, he's a nice-looking man. Is he married?" Her husband understands the disease his wife has, and that is good, especially when she introduces him to Milton.

Just as you know when someone with Alzheimer's is happy with you, you also know (and very quickly) if they're not. And if they are angry with you (or just plain angry in general), they are not above striking out and hitting you, as one lady did while I was conducting a worship service in her Alzheimer's Unit. She walked past me once, twice, then a third time. On her third pass, she reached out and hit me on the shoulder. Not very hard, but hard enough to let me know that this 89-year old woman was no weakling. "Get the hell out of here," she yelled. Some people might think that was terrible, shameful behavior. Undoubtedly, the woman who struck me would think that, too, if she didn't have Alzheimer's. To this day, I do not know what provoked her. Perhaps she thought I was a stranger in her house and did not want me there. Maybe my tone of voice or facial features reminded her of someone she didn't like. Or she could have been angry with God and saw me as a convenient substitute. Whatever it was, she acted on how she felt at the time.

Under normal social graces, many of the comments that people with Alzheimer's make would be considered inappropriate and quite rude. To those with the disease, however, their words and actions seem perfectly normal. Just ask Theodore. He simply wanted to know if that guy up in the front of the chapel was going to drink that whole cup of wine.

In dealing with Alzheimer's patients, it is best to try to maintain a sense of humor when it comes to their words and actions. As one wife whose husband has had Alzheimer's for nearly three years said to me, "If you don't laugh every now and then, you'll just end up crying all the time."

Rose

Rose's personality can be as lovely and beautiful as her name implies. On the other hand, she can also be quite prickly. When she is, you have to be careful of the thorns.

One afternoon I came upon Rose as she was wheeling herself down the hall. I soon discovered that she was trying to work out some of her anger. She had had an "accident" in her room that morning and had become quite upset when the staff did not respond to her call light as quickly as she thought they should.

"I waited and waited," she fumed. "There I was after my accident, not being able to clean up myself. It was a mess."

"How long did you wait?"

"A long time! At least twenty minutes!"

As I listened to her story, I thought perhaps her expectations were a little unreasonable. I was thinking she was just baring her thorns and being feisty again until she made a statement that was rather sobering and made me realize I was passing judgment.

"Their turn is coming," she said.

There is an old saying that I am sure most of us have uttered ourselves. "Don't judge other people until you walk a mile in their shoes." I would like to rephrase it in a way that may help us to have a better understanding of what people like Rose are trying to tell us: "Don't judge other people until you have been confined to a wheelchair or used a walker as long as they have." And certainly, "Don't judge another person until you have had an 'accident' and have had to wait for someone to come to clean you up."

Rose is right. Our turn may be coming.

Esther

At the Service of Remembrance for Esther, another nursing home resident referred to her as a dear friend and shared the memory of her as one who always explained what was physically wrong but never complained. The woman telling this, an eighty-three-year-old who uses a walker because of a hip replacement and who is in constant discomfort, emphasized the words *explained* and *complained* to make sure the members of the younger generation present understood the difference. I am not always sure we do.

I recall a conversation I had with a woman who was in her nineties. This resident had had a leg amputated several months prior and had refused to participate in special therapy during the past week. A staff person assumed she was depressed and asked me to see her. On the surface it seemed to be a reasonable judgment, especially since one of the symptoms of depression is inactivity.

When I got to the resident's room, she was sitting in her wheelchair, trying to find something in the top drawer of a nightstand. I asked if we could talk, since I had been told that she was feeling down. She said that she didn't want to go to therapy these past couple of days because she was just plain too tired. And then she said, "They don't understand the process of aging. I tried to tell them, but they simply don't listen."

Of all the concerns the elderly express to me, not having people listen is the most common. I know from over twenty-five years of counseling, the inability or unwillingness to listen is quite common. But why does it seem to be so prevalent in our relationships with older people? This may be speculation, but could part of it be the assumptions we bring with us as we enter into conversation with the elderly? "All the old people ever do is sit around and complain," or "When you get old, you just get grumpy, and when you get grumpy, you just complain." If this is part of the baggage we carry into our interactions with the older generation, then, more than likely, it will affect how we "listen" to what they are saying.

Residents have told me they have shouted because it was the only way to get someone, staff or family, to listen. It is a vicious cycle, however. They may begin by explaining but feel they are not being heard. So they yell and are heard but, because they are yelling, their behavior is often dismissed as a way of getting attention so they can complain again.

To view this now from a different angle, what would you think of someone who told you ten, fifteen, twenty times a day that her legs ache because of poor circulation. Or his eyesight is terrible due to glaucoma? Or the food needs more seasoning? Or the wheelchair needs adjusting? Would such people be seen as chronic complainers? I am afraid they would. Yet, consider: What if, for example, those who are heard as "complaining" about their legs feel they are only "explaining"? To you, it seems like all they are doing is complaining ten, fifteen times a day. Yet to them, because of short-term memory loss, they do not remember that they just said the same thing five minutes ago. For them, this is the first time they are "explaining" it.

Esther suffered from short-term memory loss. I wonder how many thought of her as a complainer. I know that none of her peers saw her as one. They remembered her as one who always explained what was wrong but never complained.

Frank

As soon as I saw the leg lying on the chair, I had to smile. Frank had gone off and forgotten it again.

Two years ago, Frank was fitted with an artificial limb after his left leg was amputated just above the knee. Being diabetic, he lost the leg because of a severe infection that could not be kept under control. The artificial limb is mainly for cosmetic purposes; he does not walk on it. Frank prefers to keep to his wheelchair. It is not unusual for him to unstrap the limb and go off in his wheelchair without it. It has been found in some unusual places and by some very surprised people.

Frank is aware that he goes off without the artificial leg and jokes about forgetting it. "Anybody got an extra leg around here?" he will ask. I think once he even told a visitor that the leg had hopped off by itself. In his joking, he is not unlike other residents who also use humor to deal with life and its circumstances.

One man in his mid-eighties told me how he came to breakfast one morning but soon realized he had to go back to his room to get his teeth. Chuckling, he said, "Yep, forgot to put them in this morning. Didn't discover them gone until I sat down and tried to eat the toast. As soon as I did, I knew something was wrong. Ever try to eat toast with no teeth?"

A ninety-seven-year-old woman laughingly said to me one day, "I just found out how old I am. It scared the tar out of me. It is lucky my memory is bad, and I don't always remember my age." That is not unlike another resident who quipped, "They told me I was ninety-nine years old today. And I thought I was an old lady at age 70!"

Frank speaks for many of the others when he says, "You can't control most of the stuff happening to you when you get old, so you might as well laugh about it."

If you ever come to visit our facility and find an artificial leg lying on a chair, don't be shocked. But most of all, don't look for someone pitying himself.

Carl

He loves lutefisk and has good-naturedly tried to get me to eat some from my very first day on the job. A big man of 100 percent Swedish blood, Carl communicates using a mixture of Swedish and English. It is not easy for me to understand him. When I first arrived, he was living in the Board and Care section of the nursing home, where residents are more independent. Over the past several years, I have witnessed his physical decline and, consequently, his move to the Chronic Care Center. In spite of increasing discomfort and pain, he tries to maintain his sense of humor, but the laughs have also declined over the years. One thing I know I can kid him about, and get a laugh, is how much he likes lutefisk. It is served several times during the Christmas season, and the residents can have all they want. Although his appetite is waning, Carl still manages to wolf down two or more servings of his lutefisk. He rubs his stomach and utters, "Ya, lutefisk. Good!" Then he points at me and asks, "You, lutefisk. Eat too?" I tell him I'm too young for that stuff and maybe next time. He laughs, "Ya. Next time! Lutefisk!"

There is, however, more to Carl than just lutefisk. In his room there is a wedding picture that hangs above his bed. It is a strikingly beautiful black-and-white photograph of a handsome young couple. Nodding to it, he talks about his wife and how much he still misses her. She died twelve years ago. They had only each other, but they did not regret being childless, for he tells me stories about how he and his wife so enjoyed life together. Both of them were hunters, and he is quite proud of the fact that she was a better shot than he. His eyes sparkle when he tells me that. You can tell he loved her and continues to love her. As we talk, tears come to his eyes. I say to him, "You really miss her, don't you?" Through more tears, he looks at me, then up at the picture, and says quietly, "Ya, I do."

There is the attitude on the part of some that when visiting the elderly in a nursing home, they should always keep the visit light and cheery. There are those who beforehand decide not to bring up the name of a deceased relative or friend because it might make the person feel sad and cry. After all, we don't want to see anyone shed tears, especially an elderly person. I wonder, when we avoid such things, who are we really trying to protect?

I recall receiving a telephone call from a family member who was agonizing about whether or not his elderly father should be told about the death of the father's youngest brother. The son asked if I thought his father should be told. As soon as I said I thought he should, the son asked, "Would you tell him?" Later I realized that this family member was having a difficult time because he himself could not handle telling his father. As it turned out, the father took the news quite well. We forget that those who have outlived most of their friends and family can have not only a perspective of how temporary life is but also an abiding faith in God.

Certainly there will be tears and sadness, as there should be. In Carl's case, the tears were there for his beloved wife, but there was also the opportunity to seize the moment to allow him to share memories. After acknowledging his sadness, I asked him to share some stories of the life he and his wife had together. He happily talked not only about their love of hunting but also about their courtship, the homes they lived in, the trips they took, and, of course, her death. As he told the stories, the tears and laughter we shared bonded us even closer.

The next time lutefisk is served, I have decided that I am going to sit down with Carl and try some. As we share that meal together, I am going to bring up his wife's name and ask if she ever ate this stuff. That day, I suspect, we are going to share some lutefisk, and perhaps again, tears and laughter. Personally, I cannot think of a better way to spend some time for both of us. Perhaps God feels that way also.

Orville

Orville never goes anyplace without it. It lies within easy reach on the tray in front of his wheelchair. You cannot walk by without hearing him say, "I got something to show you." A picture of his eight-year-old granddaughter, it is one of his most treasured possessions.

Families often express a feeling of helplessness when they see their loved ones in a nursing home. If they could do just one thing for their loved ones, I would suggest, from personal observation, that they decorate their rooms with family pictures and other personal mementos.

In our Alzheimer's Care Center, as well as in the new wings of our Chronic Care Unit, a small glass-covered case is built into the outside wall of each resident's room. It is called a "Memory Box." Families are asked to bring small items that are meaningful to, and say something about, the occupant. There are, of course, the pictures of weddings, family, grandchildren, etc. Among some of the other items I have seen displayed are an antique sugar bowl, a wooden heart with the word Grandpa painted on it, a ceramic cat, a beautiful lace fan, a replica of an old-fashioned steam engine, a pearl ring, and a tobacco pipe.

Residents who do not have Memory Boxes have their special mementos on bulletin boards in their rooms or sitting on their dressers. They love to point out these items to visitors. When asked, they are more than willing to tell the story or share the special memory each item carries with it.

It is said that a picture is worth a thousand words. Even if the item brings back but one single memory, its worth is priceless. If you don't think so, ask Orville. Better yet, ask his family.

Reminiscing

For a little over a year during my early youth, my mother and I lived in a boarding house. There are two memories from that time that I want to share with you.

The first is that of all the boarders sitting down to Sunday afternoon dinner. This was the only time during the week that everybody was together for a meal. I vaguely recall the table setting and that there were about six or seven people around the table. I distinctly remember the old-fashioned, homemade chicken noodle soup that was served. It makes me hungry just thinking about it.

The second memory is of how I, the only child at the table, listened to all those "old" people talk about things of the past. Back and forth they would go, saying, "Do you remember...," or "I remember when...," or "That reminds me...," and so forth. I wondered why all they wanted to do was talk about the past. It seemed so boring at the time. I understand now that there is a need for us to talk about, to remember, and to reflect upon the past. I have come to realize that we all do it, no matter what our age. Some people may reminisce about the Great Depression, while others spend their time reliving the rock concert they attended last month. We do it because in recalling our past, we are also making statements about who we are now.

As people of God, we are told to reminisce. For example, Ecclesiastes 12:1 tells us "to remember the God of our youth." It reminds us that the God who was with us in our youth, in our young adulthood, in middle age, is the same God who is with us in the final years of our life. When we reminisce in our spiritual life, we keep connected to the One to whom we belong and have belonged over the years.

I have heard people say that the elderly like to reminisce over and over about the same things. That is true, but is that not also true of those who express a belief in God? Is not part of keeping the faith a "reminiscing" of God's story? And in the old story is always the potential for something new.

Try this the next time you are with an older person who is telling you a story you have heard before: listen for what is beneath the story; that is, why do you think the story is important to your teller? Be aware of the feelings being expressed. Watch the person's facial expressions, and listen to the tone of voice. Ask yourself, "What is the storyteller really telling me about who this person is?" You may hear some things for the very first time.

The Snowman

"Did you see the snowman out in the courtyard?"

One morning that question was asked of me by a number of different residents. It had snowed a couple of days earlier. It was the first snowfall of the season. Wet and sticky. Perfect for building courtyard sculptures. It was obvious that those who asked wanted me to go and look. I got the sense they were eager for me to see what they had seen.

The first snowfall has always triggered memories for elderly nursing home residents. For Lucille, it is the Great Armistice Day Blizzard of 1940. "It was terrible," she recalled. "The wind and the snow. So many people died." Herbert remembers one snowy day when his father had to hitch up the sleigh and horses to take the family to church. "Dad said we couldn't miss Sunday School, and we never did." Then there was eighty-nine-year-old Dorothy, who looked out at the snow as she sat in her wheelchair and said, "Let's go out and have a good old-fashioned snowball fight. Haven't had one of those for years."

Sledding, ice-skating, making snow angels, smelling wet mittens on a hot stove, playing "King of the Hill," and building snow forts are just some of the memories the first snowfall brings to residents.

A snowman in the courtyard. I wondered what kind of memories that brought back. Did it have a carrot for a nose? Perhaps a father's smile when he saw his hat upon its head. Whatever they used for eyes and a mouth, those who live here would remember pieces of coal. Would that bring back memories of sitting around a potbellied stove? Was the snowman wearing a scarf? "Like the one Grandma knit for me when I was six years old."

"You have to go see that snowman!" said another resident.

"I am on my way," I replied.

I walked over to a window that had a view of the courtyard. Looking down, I saw the snowman with his scarf and hat. He even had a broom. But something was different. It took me a moment or two to realize what it was. He was tilting to one side. Strange, I thought. I was sure he was not built that way. Then I remembered. After it snowed, the weather had turned warm.

On the way back to my office, I crossed paths with Henry and his wife, Charlotte. Married nearly sixty years, they had come to our facility about six months ago. They were coming down the hall toward me, smiling and laughing.

"What's so funny?" I asked.

"I told Charlotte that even with her cane, she is unsteady on her feet and should lean on me for support," Henry said, still chuckling.

"And I told him he is not any steadier with his cane than I am," Charlotte said with a smile. "So we decided to lean on each other as we walked. So we've been practicing."

After they left, I went back to the window and looked out again at the solitary leaning snowman.

Almeda

Almeda is ninety-five and wants to reach 100 years of age. When asked how she plans to do it, she says, "By taking it one day at a time."

To many, taking life one day at a time is a nice philosophy. It is advertised on the T-shirts we wear or the bumper stickers we place on our cars. The words are hung on our walls using decorative plaques or placed under our refrigerator magnets. For Almeda, the words are nowhere to be seen in her room, but if you could visit with her, you would see them in her eyes.

That road to age 100 will not be an easy one for Almeda. She is suffering from a number of physical ailments. Her shoulders and arms ache constantly because of arthritis. Since she has had several falls and has fractured her hip twice, she is confined to a wheelchair. It makes no difference if she is sitting in the chair or lying in bed the pain is the same. She takes pain relievers, but they provide only temporary relief. Her doctor admits he cannot do much and tells Almeda that her body is just wearing out.

I have wondered how Almeda maintains her desire to live to be 100, knowing that it will mean continuing pain, and how she reconciles her faith with her suffering. One afternoon I asked, "Almeda, how do you hang on to your faith when you suffer so much?"

"God suffers also," she replied.

Agnes

Each day at noon I say a blessing at mealtime in six different locations. It keeps me moving, but one of the benefits is that it keeps me in contact with the residents. Besides the prayers and a few announcements, I decided to enhance the mealtime blessing by including what I call "This Day in History." It is meant to provide some fun but also to jog memories and act as a catalyst for table conversation. For example, one day I announced that it was the birthday of the composer who wrote the song, "If You Knew Suzie." That started a table of four women singing the song, with others picking it up as well. Believe me, they sang it with gusto. On another occasion, I mentioned that, "On this day in history, Congress passed a law declaring that the minimum wage was to be forty cents an hour." This prompted a discussion among quite a few of the residents about their first jobs and how much they earned. I noticed that there was interaction between staff and residents as well with that one. On the birthday of the late actor, Clark Gable, I once mentioned that having been born in 1901, he would be celebrating his ninety-fourth birthday if he were still living. No sooner had I said that than I heard Agnes, who is eighty-seven years old, retort, to the glee of the other residents and staff, "Frankly, my dear, I don't give a damn."

We need to recognize and celebrate such humor and quickness of wit among the elderly, to affirm such attributes as gifts of God and to let them know that we appreciate these gifts that they share with us. Certainly, there are residents whose dementia is such that they don't know where they are, nor do they always know their family or friends. It has been my experience, though, that even the majority of these people have not forgotten how to laugh or smile.

God works through all people, regardless of age or circumstances, to bring blessings. What is it like working in a setting with all those old people? God's blessings come anew every day through people like Agnes. What could be better than that?

Lydia

"'Humpty Dumpty sat on a wall. Humpty Dumpty had a great fall....' Do a Bible study on that," she said.

At first, I wondered if Lydia understood what she was asking. In the past month she had taken a turn for the worse and had been getting more confused. As we talked, however, she seemed to be quite clear on how much she loved to hear about God. "I love to study the Bible and God. And I remember nursery rhymes. Don't you think a Bible study on them would be nice?" Her eyes sparkled with excitement as I realized how wrong my assessment had been and replied, "Let's give it a try."

Lydia was one of the first ones there for the Bible study each week. Sitting in her wheelchair, she just beamed with a look on her face that only later I realized must have been a certain kind of pride. The studies went over very well and were greatly enjoyed by the other residents. Several of them telephoned their families to tell them what we were doing. When we finished, the residents wanted to know when we would do something like that again. Whenever Lydia's name came up, they would say, "She's that nursery rhyme lady."

A couple of months after we finished those Bible studies, Lydia died. Family members at the memorial service shared how all her life she had been an inspiration for others. One daughter said she remembered Mother deciding one year to have Christmas Eve dinner by candlelight. Lydia also thought that afterwards it would be nice if the Christmas story was read as the family gathered by the candlelight. A tradition was begun that year; one that has been kept by her children and now her grandchildren.

As we listened to the other stories about Lydia, it became clear that she had been someone who was a sower of gifts throughout her life. Wisdom, inspiration, humor, insight, and traditions were but some of the gifts she sowed. She left behind rich legacies that family and friends will continue to enjoy as long as they themselves live. And generations not yet born no doubt will also be the beneficiaries of this woman called Lydia.

As a sower of gifts, Lydia is not alone. Other residents have done, and are doing it, as well. Just because some are in their eighties or nineties does not mean the only inspiration they provide is the fact that they have lived so long. They touch and influence the lives of family and friends and staff in ways that may not always be fully understood at the time. Staff, however, will talk about Marie or Hilda or Lewis or any one of a number of other residents who have died in years gone by. They will tell you how much one's humor or another's courage meant to them. As one staff person said about a certain resident who had influenced her life, "Marie went through a lot before dying, but she always kept her dignity. She really taught me what dignity is all about. I will never forget her."

The next time you read "Humpty Dumpty Sat on a Wall...," think about Lydia and how she provided the creative idea of doing a Bible study series on nursery rhymes. She may not be with us any longer, but the seeds Lydia sowed are still sprouting.

In memory of Lydia and all the others like her who have sown seeds of inspiration and who have touched our lives even after they have completed their earthly journeys, reflect upon this: What kind of spiritual truths do you think could be learned from stories like Humpty Dumpty or Little Jack Horner or Jack and Jill or...?

Alma

Ninety-five years old, blind, and very hard of hearing, Alma spends her time sitting in her wheelchair. She tells me she is waiting to die and wonders when God will take her. "After all," she asks, "what is there left for someone like me to do?"

It took me several visits before I discovered, quite by accident, that Alma had the answer to her question literally at her own fingertips. That discovery came on the third visit when I happened to notice something under her bed that appeared to be a box cover. I was not sure what it was, so I asked her about it.

"Oh, that's my ribbon box," she replied. "I have been wondering where it has been for weeks. Can you get it for me, please?"

Picking it up, I discovered it to be filled with red, pink, and white strips of silk ribbon. They all appeared to be cut to a certain length. "What are these for?" I asked.

"Oh, they are for my roses."

The next thing I knew, Alma picked up one of the strands of ribbon and started twisting it around her fingers. She even began to hum as she worked with that ribbon. Not knowing what to expect, I just sat and watched. After a period of time, she handed me a beautiful hand-crafted silk rose. After the visit, I showed the staff at the nurses' station what Alma had made. Apparently, Alma's silk roses had found their way to others as well. A number of staff, residents, even visitors and volunteers, had received them as gifts. I learned that there were quite a few who benefited from Alma's beautiful handiwork.

The next time I came to see Alma, I announced to her, "Alma, your silk roses are everywhere! You have made a lot of people happy with them. They really appreciate them. They think the roses and you are pretty special."

I detected a slight smile on Alma's face as she replied, "Oh, they are not much. I need something to do to keep busy." And then she added, "Do you really think so?"

"Yes, I do," I replied, knowing that it was certainly true.

Alma has since died. She is no longer waiting for God to take her home. While she was waiting, however, she made people's lives a little brighter with her silk roses. I, for one, will always think of her whenever I see a rose.

I wonder how many other Almas are out there wondering what is left for them to do, other than wait around to die. It seems to me that we could do a better job of discerning and affirming the gifts they have yet to share, whether they be making silk roses, sharing stories of the past, or simply being who they are for those who want to love and value them.

I Wonder
if I Know

As chaplain, I wrote the following as a training exercise to help staff become more sensitive to the many losses people may go through when they come to live in a nursing home. The "I" in the story could be one of any number of people. It may even be someone you know.

I can remember the day I moved into the nursing home as if it were only yesterday. Our beloved President Kennedy had been shot and killed the week before, and it was three months to the day that my oldest granddaughter went out East to college. It was also the day I got my first hearing aid. Darn old thing whistled like a train.

I had lived in my home for nearly fifty-five years (fifty-three years with my husband). He died two years ago of cancer. I guess it was for the better. He had been sick for nearly two years before that. I helped him as much as I could but toward the last, I couldn't keep up with everything. I guess I am not as young as I used to be, but I'm still pretty spunky for being eighty-seven. My old high school friend, Sally, who herself went into a nursing home recently because of Alzheimer's, used to say that I had more spunk than any man she had ever seen. Of course, that's not saying much.

Before I moved I made darn sure that my family covered my rose garden so that it would be there for whoever moved in. Mary, my neighbor, will make sure they know about the roses. Mary has been a good friend. We had coffee together just about every morning. I wanted to leave my cat there also because old Buttons loved that house. You know: "Buy the house; the cat comes with it!" My son, however, did not think that was such a good idea, so he said that he would *take Buttons into his own home. Besides, it would make good company for his toy poodle. Hmmph.*

I wouldn't have had to move if my eyesight hadn't gotten so bad. I mean, I can see if the print is large enough. And gee, I was driving up to a few months ago. Until, that is, I sort of hit the side of the garage. Barely scratched the car but I sure did a good job on that old garage. Oh well, it needed painting.

They tell me at the Home I will be in one of the double rooms in the new section; E Building they call it. I wonder what E stands for. They never told me that. Probably Efficient. I hope it's clean because I took pride in my housecleaning. I enjoyed doing it. Made me feel good. I wanted to bring my old sofa, but it couldn't be done. Oh well, my son made the decision to sell it at a garage sale. I hope they got a good price for it.

They tell me that I'll love the place, and maybe I will, but I wonder if they know what I am grieving about. I wonder if I know.

Many people associate grief and grieving only with the loss of a loved one through death. Grief, however, can be multidimensional. It has been said that we are always in the process of grieving the loss of something or someone throughout our lives. Often, the elderly face a multitude of losses within a very short time span.

If you should happen to know of someone who has or will be moving into a nursing home, do some reflecting upon the losses that person may be feeling. Your sensitivity, I can assure you, will be appreciated by that individual.

By the way, what do you think the woman in the story could be grieving about?

Arthur

"I never thought I'd end up being a resident here," Arthur said.

A widower with no children, Arthur made the remark one morning just a few days after he had been admitted to the Chronic Care section of the nursing home. He was having breakfast and I had stopped by to say hello. Arthur was in his 80s, and in declining health, and he had reluctantly come to the conclusion that he could no longer care for himself at home. Actually, the conclusion was forced on him after he had fallen for the third time within a period of two weeks. The last fall scared him. Although he didn't break any bones, he lay on the living room floor in his apartment for nearly an hour before mustering up the strength to crawl to the door. He banged on the door until someone in the hallway heard him and got the apartment house manager. It was a badly bruised hip, the doctor said, and then added that perhaps it was time for Arthur to consider a place where he would receive *supervised* care. The doctor did not use the term *nursing home*—he didn't have to. Arthur knew exactly what he meant.

Arthur's remark about never imagining that he would end up as a nursing home resident is an ironic statement for one who had spent a good share of his adult life working as an assistant administrator in a nursing home. As part of his job, he no doubt had counseled many people who found the transition from their home to a nursing home difficult. I suspect he probably had said to many of those who struggled with the aging process and its consequences: "You just have to learn to accept it. You know, sooner or later, it happens to all of us. "

Having been at the giving end of care giving, Arthur now found himself at the receiving end. "I have to admit," he whispered to me after an aide had opened a milk carton for him, he was unable to open, "that it's easier giving care than receiving it. It's really hard being dependent on others." He poured the milk on his cereal and stirred it with his spoon. Adding sugar to the mixture, he tasted it, made a face, and then added more sugar. I thought he had forgotten about me standing there, until he whispered, "And do you know what, Chaplain?"

"What's that, Arthur," I found myself whispering back and then wondering why I was whispering.

"I'm suppose to get a bath this afternoon by that young woman over there." He pointed to an aide who was helping another resident with a milk carton. The aide looked over at us and smiled. Arthur continued to whisper. "Can you imagine having to depend on someone to wash you? It makes me feel like a baby." He looked over at the aide again for a moment and then motioned for me to come closer as his whispering got even softer. "Can you imagine having to have a bath by a woman?" Arthur just shook his head and took another spoonful of his cereal.

Facing the aging process and its consequences is especially difficult in a society that attempts in so many ways to deny, or at least disguise, the fact that aging is a natural part of life. At one time, it was thought that turning 40 was difficult to experience, but from my observation, more people seem to have a problem turning 30. Why? I'm not sure, but I suspect the prime reason is that when you're in your 20s, you're still considered a young adult. When you turn 30, however, you're labeled *middle aged*. At that rate, I wonder at what age are we labeled *elderly*?

I was having coffee with a group of residents one day and shared with them that I had awakened that morning feeling a little stiff. "I guess I'm getting to have my share of aches and pains," I confessed.

Sophia, who is in her 90s, laughed and said as she winked at the others, "You better be careful working here."

"Why's that?" I asked.

"Chaplain, didn't anybody tell you? Old age is contagious!"

Sophia is right. Old age is contagious, and no one is immune. And facing the inevitable process of aging will prove (to say the least) challenging. Consider, however, a comment made by Lester, a resident in his 90s who was bothered by the way the younger generation tried to stereotype him. He said with a determined look in his eye, "There's nothing wrong with me, other than I'm old."

It would be interesting to know what Arthur, now that he is a resident, would do with Lester's comment. And perhaps just as interesting, what would any one of us do with it once we had also come to the realization that old age is indeed contagious.

By the way, do you think that *you* could ever end up being a resident in a nursing home? If you can't imagine such a thing, perhaps you should talk to Arthur. He'll tell you that the aging process is full of surprises.

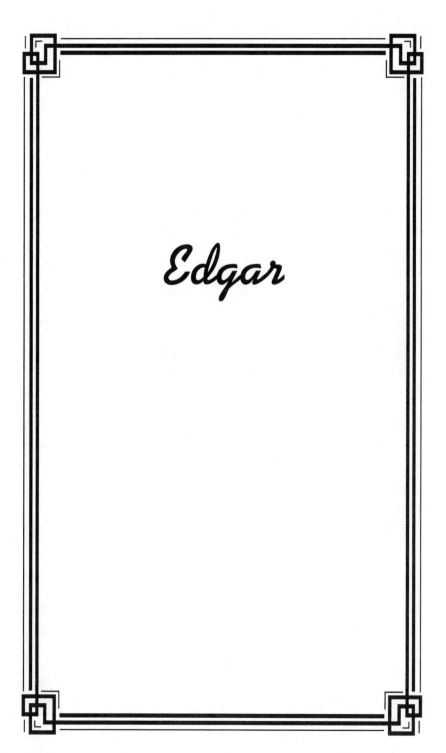

Edgar

Edgar, at age eighty-seven, refers to himself as an antique. He says he is "just like the other antiques you see walking around this place."

I have a friend who collects antiques. Antique clocks. He tells me that to be a true antique, the item should be at least 100 years old. The older it becomes, the more value it can have. I have other friends who have gathered a houseful of "collectibles," those items that are not necessarily antiques but are rare enough to be in demand.

The other day Edgar sent me a handwritten note. With no explanation, it simply consisted of verses 17 and 18 from Psalm 71:

"O God, from my youth thou has taught me,
and I still proclaim thy wondrous deeds.
So even to old age and gray hairs,
O God, do not forsake me,
till I proclaim thy might to all generations to come...."

I know there was something Edgar wanted me to see in those words. Could it be something about being an antique? I am not sure. I'm still pondering.

Joseph

I can just about count on Joseph stopping at my office two or three times a week. Although we visit and enjoy one another, I realize he is not coming in to see me. Living in the Board and Care part of our facility, he is on his way to see his wife, who has a room in the Chronic Care section. Since my office is on the way, it is used by Joseph as one of the rest stops on his journey.

"My legs are getting worse every day," he tells me as he plops himself into the chair. "They ache all the time. Poor circulation," he explains. "Runs in the family."

Joseph, one of our younger residents at age seventy-nine, needs only a cane to get around. After sitting down, he takes some time catching his breath, looking around the office, occasionally asking questions about anything that catches his eye. Once we began talking about an oil painting hanging on the wall. It shows a little boy standing on a street corner in front of a drugstore. The young lad has an ice-cream cone in one hand and a bottle of soda in the other. From the clothes and cars in the background, one can guess the painting is of a scene that dates to the 1940s. Joseph talked about being a kid and what it meant to be content, especially during the Depression. That led into a mini philosophical discussion as to what happiness is in life and whether people were happier in days gone by.

Joseph, however, does not always feel the need to talk. Once he picked up a puzzle on my desk and played with it during the whole time. On another occasion, he simply leaned back in the chair, closed his eyes, and listened to the music of Glenn Miller coming from a tape recorder.

What Joseph does in my office I see other residents doing as well as they journey throughout the facility. They also stop to take a breather, to rest as they go from one point to another. Sometimes they are in groups, chatting, while at other times, they are merely sitting together, sharing the common experience of watching others on their journeys.

Joseph never stays very long, and usually as he gets up to leave, he will say with a grin, "Well, I better get going. Had my rest."

As I watch Joseph continue his journey, I wonder: Where are my rest stops in life?

Ruth

Ruth decided that she could no longer live in her apartment and made the decision to move to the nursing home's Board and Care Unit. It was not an easy decision but a necessary one because of her continuing health problems.

"I had so many nice things in my apartment," Ruth told me during one of our first visits. "They are things my husband and I had collected over the years. But I knew when I moved here, I couldn't bring everything." After pausing to look around her room, which, she tells me, is about one-fourth the space of her apartment, she continued, "You can't have everything you want. One must let go and move on."

Years ago, I was called to a hospital to be with a family whose thirty-seven-year-old daughter was in a coma resulting from a terrible car accident. After the doctor explained to the family that their daughter was "brain dead," they turned to me for prayer. Some of them were in denial, saying such things as, "Oh, she is going to be all right," or "Let's just give it time." The doctor looked at me, and we both knew what was happening. They were hoping I would somehow say the words that would make everything okay. I quietly spoke to the family and said that we should have a prayer but perhaps it was time for a prayer for strength to let go of her and place her in God's hands. The words "let go" seemed to give them permission to face the reality. We had the prayer and then sat down as family and friends to share feelings about what they were facing.

It is never easy to let go, especially of a loved one. People like Ruth understand more than most of us what it means to let go. Like many who have lived to her age, Ruth has had to learn to let go of family and friends she has outlived, of her youth, the place she called her home, and since moving from her apartment, many of the things that were of sentimental value to her and her husband.

The residents will tell you that life never stays the same. They speak from experience. We are always letting go of something or someone.

As Ruth, at age ninety-one, says, "One must move on and make the best of it." And I know she will because it has been that kind of attitude that has brought her this far.

Wilma

Bach visits Wilma. So do Mendelssohn and Dvo-
rak. Vivaldi is no stranger. Neither are Mozart and
Haydn.

All of these composers and their music enrich the
life of a woman who seldom leaves her room because
of severe respiratory problems. On more than one occasion, I have visited her as she lay in bed with the
oxygen on and listening to a concert. The oxygen may
be helping her body breathe, but the music is helping
her soul breathe. Music has been part of Wilma's entire life. She learned to play the piano when she was in
grade school and has enjoyed playing for over eighty
years. It has only been in the past couple of years that
she has had to give it up.

As I walk by the residents' rooms throughout the
facility, I can hear anything from classical to country
western. (No, I have not heard rock yet, but I suspect
that may be coming in the years ahead.) It is not uncommon to see residents sitting in lounge chairs, feet
up, with headphones on, listening to their favorite
music.

The most popular programs offered to our people
are those featuring music: vocalists, choirs, bell choirs,
harpists, harmonicas, violins, guitars. The other day
we even had a man in his seventies entertain with the
almost lost art of making music with spoons. We also
have a number of residents who play the piano or or-
gan throughout the week at various locations.

Whenever they play, they always draw a crowd.
There are always those sitting and listening, tapping
their feet and singing along whenever appropriate. Occasionally, a couple of them will even get up and
dance.

We are very fortunate to have music therapists on staff at our facility. Music therapy reaches residents in ways that other disciplines are not always able. I have seen residents who have been unresponsive to any kind of stimuli suddenly start mouthing the words of familiar songs that are being sung to them. I have also witnessed the calming effect that music has on a resident who is visibly distraught.

Having seen the importance of music in the setting I work in, I wonder: When and if I get to the point in my life where I am living in such circumstances, what kind of music would help my soul breathe?

Gilbert

Gilbert died without carrying any grudge toward his son. Although they had had a strained relationship for over fifteen years, toward the end, it was decided they perhaps should try to get their affairs in order before "anything" happened. It was the son who took the initiative and, to his credit, bent over backward to make this happen. It was fortunate that he did. Two weeks later, his father slipped into a coma and died the following day. Both Gilbert and his son felt that for the most part, they had perhaps resolved or at least put aside the differences that had kept them apart for so long. If only all relationships would have such nice storybook endings. Unfortunately, they do not. Consider the following story.

Some years ago, I shared a hospital room with a man in his late sixties who had been diagnosed with a terminal illness. I remember one day, he gave instructions to the nurse that under no circumstances should his oldest son be allowed to visit. "If he calls, tell him I'm not here!" After the nurse left, he looked over at me and, perhaps feeling he owed some explanation, said, "We had a falling out some time ago. Haven't talked for years. Not going to, either!" Although I never did find out what caused the problem, he did tell me that he had informed his other children that their brother was forbidden to attend his funeral. "I don't even want him to know when I die."

There are no easy answers to settling family differences, especially when we are dealing with "baggage" from the past. I think, however, I might have gotten a clue the other day during a visit I had with a woman who recently came into our facility. When I asked her how she was doing, she replied, "Oh, I am doing okay." And then she made a very interesting comment that made me think of Gilbert and his son. She said quite peacefully, "I know I am traveling the final phase of my journey. I have everything I need."

When I think about life as a journey, I am reminded of stories about the early pioneers as they traveled west in their covered wagons. Their journeys were far from easy, and what often made them so difficult were all the things they tried to bring with them. I have read of how the trails they followed were littered with discarded items that were proving to be too much of a burden and were a threat to the journey itself.

We may not journey in covered wagons anymore, but there still is a lesson to be learned from the experiences of those early pioneers. Some, like Gilbert and his son, learn it. Others, like my hospital roommate, do not. I wonder what makes the difference.

Bess

After our prayer together, I said to Bess, "I will miss you." She kissed me on the cheek and replied in like manner, "I will miss you also." I walked out of her room that morning thinking those words would be the last ones she would ever speak to me.

Bess had been on total bedrest for the past six days, and no one, including herself, expected her to live. Her family had kept a vigil at her bedside for the past twenty-four hours. She was barely taking any liquids and had not had any solid food for several days. She had said her good-byes to her family and to the staff. She was at peace with God and was ready to go "home." As I write these words now, two months from the day she kissed me, you will find Bess sitting up in her wheelchair, taking her meals in the dining room, and talking with family members who come to visit.

Bess' story is not all that unusual. Nor is the opposite. On the one hand, I have seen people like Bess at death's door. Families were told they should come, only to find that the door remained closed. On the other hand, that door can open unexpectedly. A staff person told me that in the time she went out to the nurses' station to check a chart and came back to get a pen she had left in the room, the resident had died. It was completely unexpected, since a few minutes earlier, he was talking and joking as he sat in his chair, reading a magazine.

This unpredictability was described quite well in another instance by a family member. After her mother lingered on for a week when everyone was sure she would die within the hour, the daughter said to me, "You expect after you say your good-byes, the person will lay her head on the pillow, and then just close her eyes. But it doesn't happen like a movie script, does it?"

She's right. It doesn't. If it did, however, I wonder how one would like the script to be written.

John

"I want to be with him when he dies," John said as we sat in the family lounge area on the second floor of the Chronic Care Center. It was early in the morning and John had spent the night in a chair next to the bed. He had come to be with his father, who had taken a turn for the worse and had not been expected to live through the night. This was the third time within the past three weeks that John had been called in by the staff. Each time, he had spent the night. Each time, he sat and slept in that same chair. Each time, he watched his father's chest slowly rise and fall with each breath he struggled to take. And each time, his 80-year-old father survived the crisis. "He's a fighter," John told me as he sipped coffee from a Styrofoam cup. His voice reflected the tiredness shown in his face.

John has spent so much time at the nursing home over the past few months that he jokes about getting a room for himself. Like many other family members in similar situations, John is emotionally and physically exhausted from waiting for that time when death finally comes.

"I know dad is ready to go and will be at peace, but I...." John doesn't finish. He doesn't have to. I know he wants his father to be at peace, but at the same time, John is struggling with the finality of death. He is finding that the process of *letting go* is far more difficult than he thought it would be.

"Dad's always been around," John says. "It's hard to imagine what it will be like when...." His voice breaks as he gropes to find words to express himself. He takes a deep breath, sets down the cup, and attempts to rub the tiredness out of his eyes. "I just can't imagine dad not being around."

We're interrupted by a resident who wheels up to us in his wheelchair. It's Ed. He's in his 90s and very hard of hearing. I know the question he's going to ask, because he asks it every day.

"Do you think it's going to rain?" he yells.

"No, I don't think so," I yell back.

"Sure feels like rain in my bones," Ed shouts. He looks at John and nods. "If you ask me, I think it's going to rain."

Before I or John can respond, Ed wheels away. I smile at John and wink, and then resume our conversation. "I think I have a little understanding of what you meant when you said it's hard to imagine not having your dad around," I said. After my parents died, someone said to me, 'Now, you're an orphan.'"

John looks at me knowingly. "Yeah, I guess that's right. I've never thought of it that way before," he sighs. "And I'll be a 57-year-old orphan." He takes another deep breath before he speaks again. "It was hard when mom died, but at least I still had dad."

"After your dad dies," I say with some hesitation, "there's really no one left who'll remember what you were like as a child."

John nods in agreement, picks up his cup, and takes another sip of coffee. The staff had told John that the crisis appeared to be over and that his father was resting comfortably. Earlier, a nurse had stopped where John and I were having our coffee. "Your father's out of danger," she reassured him. "His condition has even improved a little." John thanked her and said that he was going to leave word at the nursing desk that he was to be called if his father's condition declined again. The nurse told him that would be fine. "I'll check back later," she said before she walked away.

"Chaplain, I should be here when he dies," John says. "Dad has always been there for me. I just wish I didn't live so far away."

"The staff is good about calling," I say.

"Yeah, they have been, and they said they would try to give me as much notice as possible."

"They will, but John, as you already know from your experience, nobody knows for sure when death will come."

John looks in the direction of his father's room. "Yeah, I know. This happened a couple of months ago when dad first got so sick. They called me and I drove down immediately. Normally, the drive would take a couple of hours. I made it in an hour and a half."

"What if you don't make it in time?" I ask.

John seems startled by my question. He looks at me for a long time before saying anything. "I can't think about that," he finally replies.

Before I say anything else, John gets up from his chair. "I think I'll go in and check on dad before I leave," he says. "I've got a long drive ahead of me, and I have to get some work done this afternoon. Besides, I gotta get some sleep."

John is representative of so many family members who feel a deep need to be with their loved ones at the moment of death. To be at the bedside when that time comes is, I feel, as it should be. However, circumstances don't always allow it to happen that way. I tell family members who feel guilty about not being at the bedside when their loved one died that one's relationship is not measured in those last few moments.

There is, however, one other aspect of this process of dying that needs to be considered. Longtime staff members say that in some cases, those who are about to die seem to want to do one last act of kindness on behalf of their families—to spare them the memory of watching a loved one die. That is why so many die in the middle of the night or early morning—times when family members are least likely to be around.

I don't know if John will be able to be there at the bedside when his father dies. I certainly hope it works out. But if it doesn't happen, I hope that we'll have a chance to have a cup of coffee together.

Walfred

Walfred is dying. He knows it. His family knows it. The other residents know it. The staff knows it.

He has been told that it is only a matter of months, maybe even weeks. A couple of times the family was called because it seemed as if it would be only a matter of hours. Although Walfred is quite religious and says, with conviction, "I know where I am going," he still admits to being afraid. Not shying away from, or feeling ashamed of, his feelings, he will talk openly about them. In particular, two fears concerning death, both of which seem to be quite common.

The first is fear of the unknown. In this life, we often experience anxiety and have questions when we are about to embark on a journey to a destination we have never been before. The same holds true for the journey we take after we die. Residents may believe they know what their final destination will be; nevertheless, there are questions. Walfred, for example, wonders what it will be like. Questions other residents have asked are: Will we have to eat food? Will I know anyone? What will be expected? What kind of clothes will I need? What will we do all the time? Will I be happy? What if I don't like it? What age will I be? Sometimes the questions themselves are quite revealing. I recall one woman who was well aware she was becoming more forgetful and confused asking, "What if I get up to the gates and don't know which way to go?"

While the fear of the unknown may be compared to not knowing what is around the corner, the second fear may be compared to going around the corner itself. It is not so much death itself that is feared but rather, the process of dying. One resident said that because of a respiratory problem, she was very anxious about not being able to catch her breath and was fearful of choking to death. In Walfred's case, he has terminal cancer and is afraid of the pain he may experience toward the end. He fears it may be too much for him and hopes the painkillers will be sufficient. He does not wish his family to see him suffering and is concerned about their emotional well-being.

During the course of a year, we have quite a few deaths at the nursing home. When residents hear of those who died peacefully in their sleep, they often remark, "That is the way I want to go." Though they also express some fear about the unknown, the overwhelming concern is always about the process of dying. They would like to have what they call "a good death"; not one that lingers on and on.

Years ago I visited a man who was dying of lung cancer, and he knew that it was only a matter of weeks. During one visit as we talked, he asked me straight out, "Would you like to know when you are going to die?" Somewhat taken aback, I hesitated for a moment. Although I had dealt with the question within various discussion groups over coffee and cookies, this was different. I replied that I had never seriously considered the question and I needed to think about it. I told him that I would let him know the next time I visited. For days I wrestled with that question and the others that grew out of it. What were my fears? What were my questions about the unknown?

I went back to share my answer and thanked him for asking the question. He nodded, and I thought I detected a slight smile when I told him how I struggled with it.

The memory of having been asked that question is with me now when I talk with people like Walfred. I think I have a better understanding that one can be religious and fearful at the same time.

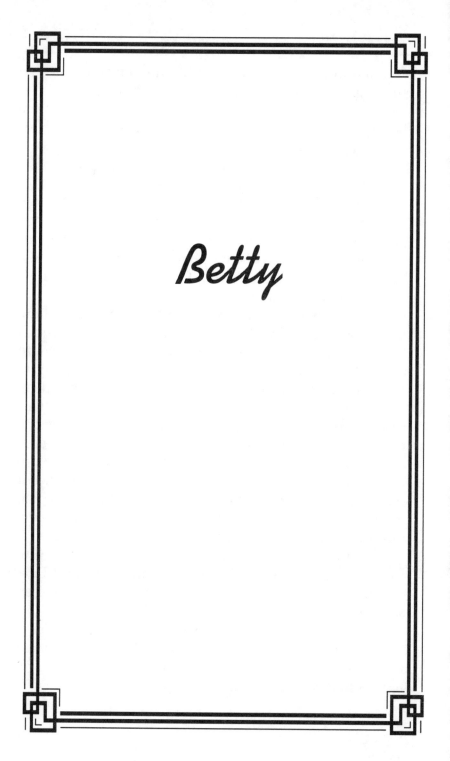

Betty

Betty just shook her head "No" when they wanted her to eat more. Even her medications, at her own request, had been stopped now for a week. She wanted to die. Having made up her mind, Betty did not want anyone to change it. She died within a month of her decision. Even though we may not agree with, nor understand, her decision, her story needs to be told.

In our first visit, I discovered Betty to be a friendly person who had always loved people and enjoyed socializing with them. According to those who knew her, she was always entertaining in her home. She was fun to be around. Now, in her early eighties, she was still mentally alert, occasionally displayed a sense of humor, and had a strong foundation of faith in God. She was, however, tired. Tired of not being able to verbally communicate because of several strokes. Tired of her wheelchair. Tired of having to be fed. Tired of being dependent. Tired of being captive to her surroundings. Tired of looking out the same window. Tired of her room. Tired.

Her last stroke left Betty paralyzed on one side, and her ability to verbally communicate had been irreversibly damaged. After months of sessions with a speech therapist, Betty reluctantly accepted the verdict. She would never regain her speech. To inquiries she could nod her head "Yes" or "No," and with staff, she communicated in that way. With other residents, however, there was very little communication, mainly due to their own speech or hearing problems. Betty indicated to me she felt isolated and knew that things would not get better.

Her decision was not made in haste, nor was it one made in isolation from God. She attended Bible study and chapel almost to the very end. The last week or so before she died, she was in bed due to her weakening physical condition and because, I believe, she willed herself to die.

When I think of Betty, I am reminded of another resident who came to the same decision because of some severe medical problems. This person, however, could verbally communicate and said to me one day, "I didn't want to tell you because I was afraid of what you might think."

Those words reflect the inner struggle of some residents. This other resident had made the decision that she did not want to suffer anymore and, like Betty, was ready to die. Both she and Betty had a strong faith and felt that God understood. They weren't sure if others would.

Emma

"Tonight I am going to die." Emma spoke these words to me and to family members who were gathered around her bed. Over the past couple of weeks she had declined quite rapidly. Emma was not in pain, but she was very weak, and her body was just plain wearing out. She was not afraid of death because she loved the Lord and had confidence that she was going home to God. She told us, "God has a room prepared for me."

Many of the residents in the nursing home talk about going home to God. People talk to me about all the deaths and ask, "Doesn't it get to be depressing?" I tell them that it is different from when I served in a suburban congregation. Most of the deaths we had in our parish were of younger people: a man in his forties has a heart attack; a young family experiences Sudden Infant Death Syndrome with their first-born; a teenager dies from an overdose; a woman, in the prime of her life, dies of cancer. In the nursing home, however, death comes at the end of a long life and is often talked about in terms of a blessing. It is a passing on to a better life. For those who are "going home," it is a celebration. They look forward to being with God and with loved ones and friends who have gone on before them. When I talk with the residents about this, I tell them there will be a sign on the gates of heaven. The sign, printed in big bold letters, will read: "No wheelchairs, walkers, bedpans, pills, etc. allowed!" Outside those gates will be a huge pile of used wheelchairs and walkers. The residents smile and nod in approval, for they understand what I mean. No wonder they look forward to going home. Such was the case with Emma.

The next morning when I came to work, I fully expected to read in the morning report about Emma's death, but her name was not on it. I knew immediately I had to go and talk with her and hear what she would have to say about still being around. Entering her room, I found her lying quietly in bed. Several family members were sitting by her side. It was a relaxed, peaceful atmosphere. Her eyes were open and there was a smile on her face. When I said to her that I was surprised to see that she was still with us, her response was, "Yes, God has a room for me, but He hasn't finished painting it yet."

Two days later, the room must have been finished because Emma died quietly in her sleep. She had gone home.

Marilla, Eben, and Otto

Marilla gave me a picture of herself the other day; a lovely photograph of her, sitting, hands folded on her lap. She is wearing a long-sleeved, velvet, emerald-colored dress with buttons up the front. There is white lace around the neck and at the cuffs. The photo captures the radiance of her personality while portraying an inner strength of character. Looking at it, one would think she was all dressed up to go someplace special. As she hands me the picture, she smiles softly and says, "This is the one I want used when I die."

Whenever our residents die, their names, dates of birth and death, and pictures of them are placed on a Memorial Board. The photographs are usually taken from the residents' charts and often are not very flattering. Such a picture would not do for Marilla. She wanted to make sure that I would have a proper one of her to display.

I recall another resident who told me that he was going to have a picture of something he wanted me to see. Nearly every day for two weeks, Eben would tell me, "It will soon be here. Just wait. I'll show it to you. You'll like it." Finally, one day a nurse informed me that Eben had something he wanted me to see. When I went to his room, he was sitting in his wheelchair, looking very pleased. "Good, you came." he said. "Here, I got something to show you." As I sat down, he handed me the photograph. It was a picture of a solid oak casket.

"Just got it in the mail this morning," he yelled, forgetting that it was *he* who was hard of hearing. "My friend took the picture a few weeks ago. He worked with me as a carpenter. Isn't it a beauty?"

Since Eben could not go to pick out a casket for himself, he had had his friend do so for him. The only stipulation Eben gave was that the casket should be constructed of wood.

Some might think that Marilla and Eben are too preoccupied with death, perhaps to the point of being morbid. Such an assumption would not be true, since, like many of their age, they are merely attempting to exercise some control over the final phases of their lives. Planning for death, at their age, is as natural as planning for anything else. They certainly do not see it as talking morbidly or giving up. It is like the resident who said to me the other day, "I've got you booked. You gotta put me away!" It was her way of saying that she wished for me to do her funeral. Assured that I would, she could be at peace and get on with life.

And then there is Otto's plan, which may present a bit of a challenge. He did not have any photographs for me to look at, but he did say, "When I finally do die, I want to be stuffed and propped up in a chair, the one by the elevator so I can watch everybody go by."

Clifford

A woman screamed as a driverless car rolled down the inclined road toward other parked cars, threatening to cause a chain reaction. Two men rushed to the car but could not get in because the doors were locked. Seeming to unfold in slow motion, this drama took place at a cemetery where I was to conduct a graveside service for Clifford.

People had just left their cars, and the pallbearers were in position as the casket was about to be removed from the hearse. Parked on an incline, the car that began rolling was third in line. We had visions of it hitting the car in front of it, causing that car to roll into the back end of the funeral coach. The pallbearers had already anticipated that scenario and were quickly stepping aside, leaving the casket in the hearse. The family watched with horrified expressions frozen on their faces.

Fortunately, the second car in line took the full impact without budging, and the crowd breathed a collective sigh of relief. The pallbearers resumed their places at the back of the hearse as the funeral director slid the casket out. Family and friends, having regained their composure, looked to me to begin the solemn procession to the grave site and reverently conduct the service. I could not help but notice now, however, that there were more than a few smiles among those gathered.

Clifford would have enjoyed the whole thing. He always told people he was somewhat of a character and always found humor in everyday situations. He was well-loved by everyone and will be missed.

Someone once said there is a fine line between laughter and tears. At the cemetery that day, we all understood that a little better.

Ebert

Ebert was considered our Christmas miracle that year.

If you know people who pretty much keep to themselves and talk only when it is necessary, then you will have a better appreciation of why we called Ebert a Christmas miracle. In his eighties at the time, he had been at the home for two years. Most of those two years were spent residing on the first floor of the Chronic Care Unit.

I had visited him off and on for over a month before I got any communication from him, and that was only a nod of his head to one of my questions. He was not suffering from dementia, and his eyesight and hearing were good. Psychologically, he was considered normal. None of these things was a factor in his not talking. I had resigned myself to the fact that he and I would never have any conversations. Then, one day, a week before Christmas, one of the nurses told me that I should go in to see Ebert. When I inquired further, she smiled and said, "Just go see him."

When I walked into his room, I found Ebert sitting in a chair, with a smile on his face. It was the first time I had ever seen him smile. Before I could say hello, he greeted me and asked me to sit down on the bed. For the next half hour he talked and laughed almost non-stop. He even got out a scrapbook and showed me pictures of a trip he and his wife took to Norway. All along I was thinking, what a dramatic change. He had such a positive outlook on life that he told me he was going to work hard at trying to walk again. His goal was to trade in his wheelchair for a walker. Finally, I managed to ask him what brought on this change. The only answer he gave me was that "something" happened to him during the night. He referred to it as a "miracle" but elaborated no further.

When I left his room I found myself checking the room number and the nameplate to make sure the resident I had been visiting with was really Ebert. After all, there have been stories about mixing up babies in hospitals. Perhaps there had been some colossal mistake and two residents were mixed up! With a more serious intent, I checked the records at the nurses' station and discovered there had been no changes in medication during the past week. This astounding change in Ebert had the whole floor buzzing. Whatever had happened to him was truly miraculous. Looking forward to visiting with him and finding out more about what happened, I made it a point to stop in several times over the next few days. Each visit was greeted by this outgoing, friendly, gregarious man. He never elaborated on his transformation. He only repeated that something miraculous had happened to him that night.

Two days before Christmas I stopped at Ebert's room. I was going to ask him to show me more of the pictures of his trip to Norway. When I walked in, he was lying curled up in his bed. He was not smiling, and he appeared to have reverted to his former self. Although I tried to engage him in conversation, he did not speak a word. The only way he acknowledged my presence was by glancing up at me every now and then. After I left, I went to the nurses' station to inquire what happened. They said that he had been like that since the previous night. Having gone to his private little world, he remained that way until he died a year later.

Residents often ask me questions that touch upon the mysteries of life and death. Why have I lived so long? Why does he have to suffer? Why did she linger so long before death? Why are there terrible diseases such as Alzheimer's? In responding to such questions, I often use the illustration of a booth in heaven. I ask them to imagine this booth and that it has a large sign above it announcing in big, bold letters, "All Questions Answered Here!" Sitting in that booth will be God. At that time all our questions will indeed be answered. No doubt, there will be a long line of people waiting to ask God some questions they have wrestled with all their lives. I also tell them if they get to heaven first, to save a spot in the line for me, for I have a few questions myself. One is about a person named Ebert and a certain Christmas miracle.

Harry

The only verbal greeting Harry has ever given me has been in response to my saying, "Shalom, my friend." He smiles and replies, "Shalom." Harry has dementia and spends his time shuffling up and down the corridor of the second floor in the Chronic Care Center. Those who knew him before the onset of his dementia tell me he is only a shadow of the man he once was.

It is not easy for family members or friends to witness the changes their loved ones go through as dementia takes its toll. Along with the physical effects of the aging process, the mental and personality changes can be overwhelming. It is hard to watch a person you have known all your life as intelligent and articulate who now can only babble incoherently. Or to see a person who took pride in his own independence be forced to depend upon others to feed him and lift him in and out of bed. Or to accept that a gentle person has become verbally and physically abusive.

I certainly do not intend to minimize the agonizing pain that comes from watching a person slip into this shadow-like being of the person he or she once was, but I ask you to reflect upon a thought that may give a small measure of comfort: It may not be as difficult for the person who is experiencing dementia as it is for the person on the outside looking in. I offer as an illustration a personal experience I had when I was young.

When I was fourteen, I came down with a severe case of influenza. It hit me so hard that I was out of it for four days. Aching all over and moaning out loud, I would ramble on, saying things that did not make sense. At times, I even hallucinated. My sheets and pajamas were changed a couple of times a day because they would be soaked through with sweat from the high fever. I was led to the bathroom and back. I was spoon-fed Jell-O and often spit it out or dribbled on myself.

It was a terrible time; at least, so I have been told. Personally, I do not have any memory of the experience, other than the beginning stages and the last after the worst was over. It was only after I recovered that I found out from my mother how I behaved. I may have been back to normal, but my mother was physically and emotionally exhausted.

I realize those suffering from dementia may not get better. It is not my intention to minimize the anguish that condition causes for their loved ones and friends. Again, I offer a thought that might be of some comfort. It is worse for those on the outside trying to look in than it is for those on the inside who no longer can look out. I can only think of Harry and his greeting of "Shalom." There is a peace about him.

I believe in God and also that there is more than this one life. When the time comes for Harry to be awakened by his Creator, I can imagine God telling him how sick he was and Harry's response: "Really? I don't remember."

Cecil

Cecil lost his wife three years ago. They had been married for sixty-five years. At the time of her death, Alma was on the second floor of the Chronic Care Unity Center. Cecil was living in the Board and Care section of the facility. Although the buildings are connected and thus there is no need to go outside from one building to another, Cecil still had a distance to travel to see his wife. For any staff person, walking at a brisk pace from Cecil's room to his wife's room would take six to seven minutes. Cecil, however, had trouble with his legs. They ached all the time and he required a walker to get around. For him, a trip to see his wife was no small journey; but make it he did, at least once a day. On any given day, one could walk past him as he sat in a chair renewing his energy before traveling another twenty or thirty feet to his next rest stop. No one needed to ask him where he had been or where he was going, for his steadfast devotion to his beloved Alma was well-known by all.

Cecil was a likable fellow. He had a way about him that was gracious. Friendly and outgoing, he had a kind word for everyone. His persona bestowed the grace of God. It was hard to explain how it happened; it just happened. Some might talk about it in terms of a kind of mystical, spiritual experience as one would perhaps describe an encounter with a "holy man." Considering Cecil's easy-going manner and infectious smile, however, a "down-to-earth" angel might be a more accurate description. One day, for example, he took a fall when his feet got tangled up with his walker. He, of course, was on his way to see Alma. Three staff immediately came to his aid as he lay on the floor. As they knelt beside him, they were all concerned about a possible fracture. Cecil, however, looked up, and with a smile he said, "Call a tow truck." Fortunately, he did not break anything, but even if he had, Cecil would have, in his own way, bestowed grace upon those who came to assist him.

When we passed in the hallway, Cecil sometimes made the sign of the cross as a greeting. He did this with such elegance that no words were needed. It was just another way in which he manifested grace and bestowed the blessings of God upon all who crossed his path. When his wife died, he was at her bedside and held her hand for a long time afterwards. He again showed his graciousness by making sure he thanked all those who were involved in helping to take care of his Alma.

Cecil died a year after Alma's death. The spirit of graciousness with which he so blessed those around him, however, lives on. The next time you visit someone in a nursing home, don't be surprised if grace is bestowed upon you by those who live there. Who knows? You just may be fortunate enough to cross paths with someone like Cecil.

Jacob

"Do you bless angels?"

The question came from Jacob as he stood in the doorway of my office. He looked hesitant about coming in, as if unsure of my response to such an inquiry.

Jacob is in his late sixties. He lives in the Assisted Living section of our facility. While he had been a resident for just a little more than a month, he had already paid me several visits during that time. In previous visits, he would come in, sit down, and chat about anything and everything. He was always amiable and jovial, often sharing humorous stories about his experiences working for the railroad. "Worked for the trains for nearly fifty years," Jacob told me during our first visit together. "And I've got lots of railroad stories to tell." But on this visit, I immediately sensed that it would be different. There would be no train stories today. When he appeared at my door that morning, his countenance told me that he had not come simply to chitchat. He was on a quest, and it had to do with angels.

"I'm not sure what you mean," I replied as I motioned for him to come in and have a seat. He stood there for awhile, and I figured he was pondering whether or not he should come in. Finally, he nodded his head, indicating to me that he would accept my invitation. Using his walker, he slowly shuffled to the front of my desk and stood, his hands resting on the walker.

"Why don't you sit down," I said.

He neither sat down nor replied. I waited and then watched as he steadied himself with one hand on his walker while his other hand fumbled in his shirt pocket. After a bit of a struggle, he extricated something wrapped in what appeared to be many layers of tissue paper. He released his grip on the walker so he could use both hands, but he became unsteady and had to grip his walker again. At that point, he decided to sit in the chair I had offered. My curiosity intensified as I watched him carefully unwrapping the tissue paper. Because of his initial question, I had an idea of what might be inside. My suspicions were soon confirmed when he uncovered a beautiful figurine angel. It was a young girl with golden hair and wings. Her angelic face, delicately painted, reflected serenity and peace. After stuffing the tissue paper back into his pocket, Jacob gently set the figurine on my desk.

"Can you bless this?" he asked quietly.

I picked up the figurine to look at it more closely, and then replied in a respectful tone of voice, "Is this something like your guardian angel?"

"Yes, you can call it that." Jacob cleared his throat as he watched me look at his angel. "Chaplain, I have a tough decision facing me tomorrow morning at the doctor's office. I'm going to need all the help I can get. My sister gave the angel to me last week when she came up to visit. She said it would watch over me."

He cleared his throat again, and I asked him if he needed a glass of water. "I'll be alright," he said. "Anyway, Chaplain, I have carried that angel with me wherever I go. In the evening when I go to bed, I put it on my night table. It's the last thing I see at night and the first thing I see in the morning."

Although my seminary training never prepared me for the blessing of angels, I knew what I was going to do. I had made my decision when I invited him into my office. I knew I was about to venture into uncharted spiritual waters, and I wondered what some of my professors would say.

"Jacob, I'd be happy to say a prayer and give a blessing for your angel," I said.

"Thank you, that would mean so much to me," he whispered. Without saying another word, Jacob closed his eyes and bowed his head. He was ready.

I picked up the figurine and held it in the cup of both hands. My prayer was short and to the point. I asked God to bless this angel and have her watch over Jacob as he faced his journey ahead. After I finished I noticed that Jacob still had his head bowed. As I waited for him to finish what I figured were his own silent prayer and blessing, I realized that I did not even know Jacob's religious background. But then I decided that it didn't matter when it came to the blessing of an angel.

Angels play an important role in the lives of many of our residents. In addition to the figurines I see sitting on shelves in their rooms and guardian angel pins worn on their blouses and suit coats, there are stories of angels that residents have shared. One woman talked about how when she thought she was going to die, she saw an angel sitting at the foot of her bed. The angel didn't say anything, but the next morning, the staff members were all amazed by the woman's remarkable recovery. On other occasions, staff members have shared with me that they have cared for dying residents who spoke of having seen angels just before they died.

Several days after Jacob had made his request, he stopped in the doorway of my office.

"How'd it go?" I asked.

Jacob didn't say anything. He didn't have to. He simply smiled and patted his shirt pocket.

Beatrice

"I was afraid you wouldn't find me." Those were Beatrice's first words to me. She had that very day been transferred to the Alzheimer's Care Center from the Board and Care section of the facility. We have a sixty-bed center that is divided into three wings of twenty beds each. Residents are placed in a wing according to the stage of the disease. Beatrice's room was in the wing that housed those in the early stages. She was in her room, sitting in a rocking chair and looking out the window. We had had contact with each other when she lived in Board and Care, and though my name always eluded her, she recognized me as the chaplain. I had come now to see how she was adjusting to her new home. Appearing anxious, she took my hand and held on tightly as she spoke those initial words.

A soft-spoken, attractive woman, Beatrice has short-term memory loss and confusion to the point where she can no longer be responsible for herself. She knows she is losing her memory, and it frightens her. That is one of the sad things about the beginning stages of this disease. The patients often do realize what is happening but are powerless to do anything about it. They know they are becoming more forgetful and are just trying to hang on to what they can remember. Equally important is that they, too, be remembered. They need to be reassured that they are not being forgotten.

Beatrice's words stayed with me throughout that week as I turned them over and over again in my mind. I realized that what she said was less a statement to me as a person and more to what I, as a chaplain, represented. Or rather, I should say, "Who" I represented. It is not difficult to imagine that those with this

disease might feel as if they are sinking into the darkness of a black pit. One of the spiritual struggles they
face is that perhaps even God will not be able to find
them.

Just as we often need reassurance that God is with
us, those with Alzheimer's also need to hear that no
matter where their journey might take them, they will
not be lost to God. That truth made itself known to
Beatrice and others one morning during a worship
service held in the wing on which she was a resident.

We began the service, as we always do, with music
and song. Nursing home residents love to sing, and
though they may have forgotten many things, they
seem to remember the words to many of the old-time
hymns. Since there is very little material available in
the area of providing worship services for those suffering from Alzheimer's, we like to experiment cre-
atively. One thing that has proven to be effective is the
use of posters portraying animals or little children.
Each poster bears a brief caption. One week we used a
poster that showed a kitten sitting in a thicket. The kitten appears to be lost and has the look on its face of
wanting to be found. The caption read, "God hears
even the smallest voices." When the poster was
shown to the group, one of the men looked at it for a
few moments, read aloud the caption to the rest of the
residents, and then commented with a spiritual insight
that would match the best of those uttered by any the-
ologian. "Well, that must mean He hears our voices
also." Almost all the residents who were there that
morning, including Beatrice, responded to that statement by either saying "Yes" or nodding their heads in
agreement.

Beatrice was reassured that day by another who suffers from the same disease. The question is, How will she be reassured tomorrow or the next day? Or how will she be reassured when she moves into the more advanced stages of the disease? None of us knows for certain, but staff, family, and friends will do whatever they can. And when we ourselves feel discouraged and helpless and wonder if she feels all alone in that darkness that we are not always able to penetrate, there is a poster of a small kitten that might provide a comforting insight.

Six Words

Recently, I just may have had a visit from an angel!

Frequently I come back to my office after visiting with residents or staff, and I find that someone has left something on my desk. It is usually an article or a clipping that the person thought I might enjoy. Sometimes the givers leave their names, but not always. This past week, a business card containing six words was left on my desk. I have no idea whom it came from, but the words are worth sharing. I think they can sum up a worthwhile philosophy of life. The card reads as follows:

Live Well • *Laugh Often* • *Love Much*

A philosophy of life, yes, but more. We can gain much by reflecting on what those words can mean when we put them together with a spiritual foundation. Imagine God saying these words to us. Perhaps the messenger was an angel leaving God's business card. If that were the case, what then would these words mean? How can we put them into practice in our current circumstances? In the relationships we have now? In the day-by-day living we do?

As I said, I don't know who left the card, but it could have been an angel. I suspect it could even have been an "elderly" angel.

If it is God's business card, what do you think God is telling us? Could it have anything to do with visiting someone in a nursing home? Could it be related to the verse from the Bible that says, "Do not neglect to show hospitality to strangers, for thereby some have entertained angels unawares?" (Hebrews 13:2)

A Final Thought from the Author

Although these stories about the elderly were written to help us rethink whatever stereotypes we may have, they also serve to affirm that each person is a unique creation of God. To fully understand that truth, we need to look beyond their wrinkles. When we are willing to do so, I believe our lives will be blessed because we will then have the privilege of experiencing them for the individuals they are: children of God who laugh and cry and love and hurt and hope, just as we do.

Whenever we can draw upon the wisdom and insight of those who are traveling in the last phase of their earthly journey, we may be better prepared to begin that part of the journey ourselves.

It is my hope that you will want to revisit these stories from time to time, and that the individuals within them might become traveling companions as you continue your journey through life.

An Invitation to the Reader

Many of you have stories similar to the ones I have related. They may be about a grandparent, parent, spouse, distant relative, friend, or even about yourself. These personal experiences of courage and wit and faith need to be shared so that all of us will understand that the aging process need not diminish the human spirit nor the uniqueness of each individual. I would be privileged to hear your story.

Chaplain Chuck Tindell
P.O. Box 240561
Apple Valley, MN 55124

Order Form

Please Send Me:

_____ copies of *Seeing Beyond the Wrinkles*
    @ $12.95 per copy   _____

_____ copies of *Study Guide* @ $4.95 per copy   _____

California residents add 8.25% tax   _____

Postage & handling for one item   ___$2.50___

Postage & handling for additional
    items @ 75¢ each   _____

TOTAL ENCLOSED   ==============

Payment Type

❏ Check   ❏ Money Order   ❏ Visa

❏ Mastercard   ❏ Discover   ❏ American Express

Credit Card #: _____ Exp. Date: _____

Name: _____

Address: _____

City: _____ State: _____ Zip: _____

Make checks payable to:

Studio 4 Productions
P.O. Box 280400
Northridge, CA 91328-0400
U.S.A.